Juggling

1 *8* *1* *7*
HARPER & ROW, PUBLISHERS
Cambridge, Philadelphia, San Francisco, London, Mexico City, São Paulo, Sydney
NEW YORK

Juggling

a novel by

Robert Lehrman

FIRST EDITION

Library of Congress Cataloging in Publication Data
Lehrman, Robert.
    Juggling.

    Summary: High school soccer star Howie Berger struggles to cope with the vagaries of first love and to win the respect of his clannish teammates on the club team.
    [1. Soccer—Fiction]   I. Title.
PZ7.L53275Ju 1982   [Fic]   81-48654
ISBN 0-06-023818-6   AACR2
ISBN 0-06-023819-4 (lib. bdg.)

To Susan

One

1

You put the sole of your foot on a soccer ball, roll it back onto your instep, and with a little flip of the ankle, send it into the air. Then you see how long you can keep it up. You use your feet. You use your thighs. You send it high, arch your back until your forehead is underneath the ball like a table, and, if you time it right, you can keep the ball bouncing off your head forever. They call this "juggling," and nobody could juggle like I could.

This was a time when soccer wasn't exactly the biggest sport on Long Island. Which I liked.

"Let the big guys go out for football," I had told Alfred, my best friend, when we were in eighth grade. "I'll play soccer. Be a *star*, man."

My father had played semipro for a Jewish team in Hamburg before escaping from Germany in 1938, and for a few clubs around New York until he turned forty. He worried I would think there was something unmanly about the fact that he was awkward at American sports; when I was ten he took me, an only child, to games played by immigrant teams in Brooklyn and showed me the sports pages of foreign papers ("Look! In England, that's all they care about!") to convince me that playing soccer took guts. When everybody else's fathers were pitching baseballs to them in their backyards, he threw soccer balls to me and gave me nickels if I could head the ball back to him twenty times in a row.

It worked. After school in the winter I would go to the locker room, change into the blue shorts we wore for gym class, and go onto the floor. When I was a junior I could juggle almost five minutes at a time. Kids still changing after eighth-period gym class would bring their briefcases into the gym and watch. "That's Berger," I would hear them say, soberly. "He's good."

I made like I didn't notice. But if there were girls around I would let the ball drop, and send a hard, low shot, sounding like a small cannon, against the gym wall. Then I would jog after the ball, flip it into the air off my instep and go to work again, a skinny-chested kid with long, black hair slicked back into an Elvis Presley DA, with thighs and calves so big, Mr. Dillon, the track coach, once saw me in the locker room and said, "Those aren't calves, Berger. Those are cows."

○ ○ ○

A jet coming in from the Atlantic would have passed less than a thousand feet over our house before coming in to land at what in 1960 was called Idlewild Airport. The Five Towns were on the south shore of Long Island. Our town was Cedarhurst, in whose curving back roads were pockets of Wasps, families with blond kids who jammed tennis rackets into their bike baskets and never went to the public schools. Inwood was the slum; blacks and Italians lived there in uneasy coexistence.

But most people in the Five Towns were Jews. Not only that, they were *rich* Jews. Not only that, they were *newly* rich Jews with a reputation for crassness we had to defend even in high school. They spoke without *R*'s and with glottal stops and the inflections of Brooklyn and as if everyone were deaf. They drove Cadillac Eldorados with monogrammed initials on the driver's door, came back from Florida—from the Fontainebleau—each January with leathery tans. When their son turned sixteen he got a Corvette. When the daughter turned sixteen she disappeared for two weeks, returning to school with the shadowy remnant of two black eyes and a delicately sculpted replacement for the big honker that had made her cry each time she looked in her Tru-lite makeup mirror.

Among my friends it was fashionable to say we hated the place. We defended living there on the grounds that we were being stereotyped. "We got kids, they're going to Harvard," I would say to my cousins from Roslyn. "We got one girl, she's a *pianist.* Classical." Actually, we liked being stereotyped. There was something exciting in knowing people thought we were all like Steve Perlman, who, when his parents left for Florida, held a two-day party which had emptied his parents' liquor cabinet, and in which someone had thrown a chair through the picture window in the living room. And got *away* with it! When his parents came back, they just laughed and fixed things up! And what about the Peskins, Mort and Marty, twins, who a year ago had cashed two thousand dollars of their Bar Mitzvah bonds and lost it all in a week of betting at the Big A? Crude, sure. But daring.

The problem was that my parents didn't have the money to laugh at chairs thrown through picture windows, and that made me uncomfortable with the kids who had. But there was nothing uncomfortable about being daring on the soccer field. By junior year I was a star. There were trophies and plaques covering my bedroom wall to make that clear: All-County for two years; MVP for the Lawrence High School Golden Tornadoes; high scorer for the county, sophomore *and* junior years. On a shelf above my bed was a brown leather ball with *LHS 4, Massapequa 2* scrawled across the stitching in white shoe polish. I had scored all four of those goals to win us the league championship, and when I graduated, the ball would go into the trophy case that took up the wall across from the principal's office at school.

By junior year I was good enough to be dissatisfied with simply being a high school star. Of course I could trap a ball, outfake a defender, and dribble through high school fullbacks like they were statues. American boys couldn't care less about soccer; they swapped baseball cards and dreamed about Johnny Unitas, not Pelé. Most of the players on my team hadn't seen a soccer ball until they entered junior high.

How could I become good enough so I could go over, say, to England, where First Division games drew a hundred thousand people? Where I could play before crowds for whom simply being an American would be incredible ("A Yank? Did they say he's a Yank?"), and where announcing my name would bring a roar from the packed concrete benches of English stadiums?

When I began talking like this to my father, he actually got mad.

He was an "executive" for a perfume company. At least, that was the way I used to describe what he did. I knew he was a "success"—not as much as Steve Perlman's father, not wealthy, but someone who was "doing well." I thought of him as a stern father. He rarely talked about his job. Later, when I met some people who had worked with him, I was surprised to find that not only did they respect him—he wound up as an assistant vice-president in marketing—they had liked him very much because of his "way with people." He was a tall, balding man who loved America, worked very hard to eliminate his accent, and was surprised and a little chagrined when people said they noticed it.

"Ridiculous," he said, when I asked him about England. "Why?"

"In America you got the best medical schools in the world. *Har*vard. Col*um*bia. Be a doctor. Then when you're forty you're not washed up. There's no money in soccer. Not in America."

The more I talked, the more he argued. Soccer was fine for a boy; he wanted me to go to a fine eastern school, major in biology, go to labs all afternoon, and put soccer in its place. He wouldn't play with me anymore, and in the fall of junior year, when he discovered me reading a book on soccer tactics after I had announced I was doing homework, he pounded his fist into the palm of his other hand. "That damn game," he said. "I wish I never introduce you to that damn game." From then on he stopped going to my high school games.

I didn't understand. After all, he had pictures of himself in soccer uniforms framed and hanging in the basement. He had described to me the way he would cut school in Bremerhaven, where he had lived, and head for the soccer fields, where he would stay all day. Did that mean he was washed up? In fact, I wanted to be a doctor and already had the Cornell bulletin on the shelf above my desk. But where I really wanted to study pre-med was St. Louis.

St. Louis! Home of St. Louis University, NCAA champs two years in a row! The only school in the country where soccer was big-time; where you could walk through the dorms and have people point you out because you could shoot with both feet! If I was at St. Louis I could play with ballplayers as good as me. I could practice indoors in the Fieldhouse because St. Louis alone among American schools reserved time for soccer all year round.

And if the school was famous, even more famous was its coach, Walter Perkins, a picture of whom, sitting implacably on the bench, legs crossed, puffing at his pipe during the climactic moments of a championship game, was the indispensable illustration of *New York Times* soccer coverage.

Perkins had played for St. Louis in the thirties, and it was he who had built the entire St. Louis program so there were youth leagues and clinics and camps like in no other city in the States.

He took almost every one of his players from the St. Louis area; he hadn't had a New Yorker on his roster for ten years. But wasn't there always a first time? I sent for the St. Louis catalog. And when my father saw it curled inside the mailbox we had our biggest fight.

"No," he said as we sat down to dinner.

"Please?"

"We can't afford it."

"I could get a job there. Get a job, try out for the team. I know I can make it."

"Gottamn it," my father said. Whenever he was angry his accent thickened. "I'm sorry I ever introduce you to that dumb game. You're going to be a doctor, not a bum."

"I can learn to be a doctor in St. *Louis*."

"A school for mediocrities. Are you mediocre? No. You can play for Cornell."

"I play for Cornell, I can't get the training I need."

"For what? Look, you are a good player. *As an American.* But there are a million English kids as good as you. A million German kids as good as you. Not because the little Nazi bastards are smarter or bigger or stronger or faster. But because they play soccer every day of their life from five years old and they see the best players in the world all the time."

"Dad, why do you *say* this?" I said. *"Why?* You haven't seen me play in *months.* I'm *better.* I'm *pass*ing good. I'm *mov*ing the ball. I see ahead."

He said nothing.

"Just come to one game! Watch me!"

My father looked down and, to indicate the subject was closed, picked up his spoon and began picking the maraschino cherries out of his fruit salad and placing them with distaste on the saucer.

Still, he didn't forbid me to apply. I did, hoping if I got a scholarship to St. Louis he might change his mind. He didn't make me drop off the team at Lawrence either, and at the end of the junior year, in 1960, he even let me try out for Maccabiah, an all-Jewish team of immigrants who played in the roughest amateur league in New York and had finished second three years in a row.

The champs were usually Hercules, the Greek team. There were also a Jamaican team, three or four varieties of Latins, a French team, and an English team. Only the English team spoke English on the field. The players lived in Queens, Brooklyn, or Long Island, but they played games at Hempstead State Park on a field whose grass was worn thin by May, a month after the season opened.

The Maccabiah coach was Aaron Gatch, a little man with thinning, curly gray hair. He had played for the United States in the World Cup, ten years before, the one in which we beat England; Gatch was fifty, taught gym at a junior high, liked to play with the second team during scrimmages, and was wearing shorts and cleats when I showed up to try out one day in June.

2

"*Howard* Berger," he said. "I know the name."

"From *Newsday*," I said. "I play for Lawrence High."

"That's right. You play wing."

I knew I should sound modest, but I couldn't help it. "I can play anywhere," I said.

He raised his eyebrows. "Ah," he said. "Good."

He kicked a ball around with me for five minutes, then let me scrimmage on the second team while he stood on the sidelines and watched me learn my lesson.

Because as I raised my foot for the first ball that came my way it was picked off by a big man who cut in front of me. I trapped the next ball, gave my defender a fake left, went right, and ran into his foot set squarely in front of the ball.

Now I was nervous. The next time I got the ball I looked up, and all my teammates were covered. Out of the corner of my eye I saw a fullback coming out on me. I could have screened the ball from him. Instead I crossed it wildly into the middle.

"*Paz* de ball," one of the reserves called to me. "Don't piss it avay."

He was angry at me! A goddamn *substitute*! But the next

10

twenty minutes were no different. The play was just too fast for me. When I came to the sidelines I smiled at Gatch with the guilty smile of somebody who has been caught in a lie.

But he was smiling. "Not bad for an American," he said. "Good left foot. Nice moves. We can use you. Not to play, we got a strong first team. But we can let you scrimmage. Let you suit up for games. After that, who knows? You grew up in an army base, maybe?"

"My father taught me," I said. "He's German. A Jew, but German."

"Ah, the father. Tell him he did a good job."

It surprised me; my throat swelled and all I could do was nod and turn away. That night, when my mother asked, "How did you do today?" I thought about telling my father on the chance that his face would crease into a smile the way it did when something pleased him. I glanced toward the table; he was helping himself to more pot roast, careful to look oblivious. I suddenly realized that even if he was pleased he wouldn't let me see it. I shrugged. "I made the team," I said.

After dinner I went to the front porch and stood looking out at our neighbors walking dogs and arranging sprinklers on their lawns. It was still light. I thought about taking a walk through town until I calmed down enough to shrug off his indifference. Only now something else was bothering me and it wasn't soccer.

It was spring. That meant the streets were filled with kids like Mort Peskin, driving down Central Avenue in Corvettes, one arm around a girl. George's, the candy store on Central Avenue, would be filled with them, meeting for ice-cream sodas, then sitting for hours at the Formica tables in back, giggling loudly, blowing soda straw wrappers at the ceiling.

11

It was as if every boy in the Five Towns was with a girl except me. I had a varsity jacket and two letter sweaters. But I hadn't asked any girl out. Ever. In three years of high school I hadn't had one date.

Until last year I could tell myself this was something I would outgrow. Someday wouldn't I turn my attention to girls and learn to handle them the way I had learned to juggle? But a few months ago Alfred, after three years my best friend still, had started going out with Barb Olman; every evening after dinner, instead of coming over to my house, he would head for hers so they could do homework together. And now, sitting alone on the porch, with no one to call, I realized that it wouldn't be long before I would have to find a girl myself, and it wasn't going to be like juggling at all.

o o o

The idea petrified me. Calling a girl up and having to make small talk; picking a movie she liked; knowing about how to open doors and pay for checks and when to put your arm around her in the movies, and how you could properly broach the matter of a midnight drive to the tennis courts in Atlantic Beach where seniors who had their driver's licenses would park—the whole thing seemed so complicated it was simpler to think about soccer all the time and jerk off to copies of *Dude* and *Gent*.

I had worried about this the summer of sophomore year, which I had spent as a Good Humor man, and during which I met Alexandria Robinson, a chubby, kinky-haired sophomore from Long Beach who would come out of her house, buy two toasted almonds, and walk me through half my route.

One night she stayed with me as I turned up Shore Road, where there were only a few houses and no streetlights and where it seemed natural to put my arm around her.

She moved closer against me. I put my hand on her breast and, when she made some kind of moaning noise, turned toward her, kissed her, and started to put my hand down her bermudas.

She moved away and gave me a smile even I could see was meant to be friendly. "Let's save that for next time," she whispered.

Next time? Did that mean we would have to start "going out"? Did that mean I would have to start calling her and taking her to restaurants and showing her how awkward I was in everything that really counted? That night I came back to the Good Humor plant and walked into the manager's office.

"Can I change my route? There's this girl bugging me."

The manager, a man whose nose was red and rough and who only got up from his desk to go home, swiveled his chair around to look at the map. "We can put you in Atlantic Beach. McNamara's quitting."

"I'll take it."

"What do you mean, bugging you? You mean she's after you? That what you mean?"

"They're all after me," I said. And left before he could explore the accuracy of that little bit of juggling with facts.

○ ○ ○

But afterward I was disturbed. Was this normal? To turn down a perfectly willing girl who wanted me inside her blouse before I had taken her to the movies?

The funny thing was, I knew girls liked me. They laughed at my jokes in English class, Patricia Koplowitz and Bonnie Levick showed an inordinate interest in soccer for about three months each, and Michele Baumgartner had embarrassed me by writing a note in math class about my "sexy" legs; Mr. Graumann had intercepted it and horrified her by reading it aloud. I was horrified, too. Since Mr. Dillon's joke I had become sure my legs were disproportionately big. I wore long pants in the summer and had refused a full-length mirror for my bedroom.

Was I shy because of my looks? No. Sometimes, when the DA was freshly combed, when the spit curl hung just right and I was wearing my leather jacket, black penny loafers, and white socks, even I liked me.

Was it because I was a virgin? No. There was occasional talk of the miracle girl who "did it"—Elaine Keane, for example, who was rumored to do "two at a time." But most of us were virgins. Besides, the girls I had crushes on were Jewish and going to college, and for them progress was measured in smaller steps. "Bare tit," I heard Jonathan Mandelbaum say, disgustedly, one Monday morning about his girl. "Bare *tit* after three *months.*"

Jewish girls didn't do it. They gave you *hand* jobs. They let you touch them all over if you were going steady. But they were virgins and so were the boys. Alfred was a virgin. Probably even the Peskins were virgins. Losing my virginity could wait. All I wanted was to touch some girl's nipple and feel it stiffen the way I had read about in *A Stone for Danny Fisher.* In fact, it would be nice to have someone just to go to the movies with and afterward drive home, talking about life and not even touching at all, at least for the first few weeks.

I had no idea what made me so shy. But suddenly, these days, I was terrified that I could turn out like cousin Abe, my mother's first cousin, a skinny, stoop-shouldered Caspar Milquetoast who, at forty-five, still lived with his sister,

14

worked in a knitting mill as a clerk, and, at family parties, sat, his legs crossed at the knee ("The way fags do," my cousin Michael said), a sexual neuter, smiling vacantly, listening to others and afraid to open his mouth.

And now, as I sat down in the porch, a screened-in affair with cast-iron porch furniture fitted with green plastic cushions, Alfred pulled up in the 1952 Plymouth he had bought for fifty dollars. He walked up the gravel driveway.

"I'm on the porch," I called out.

"Oh. Great. Didn't see you," he said.

3

Alfred was not interested in sports at all. We were best friends because we went to Camp Ramah together, because we were editors of the grade school yearbook, and because his house was two blocks from mine and in summer it was easy for him to walk over with a half-gallon of Breyer's banana fudge ice cream and sit on the porch with me while we polished it off.

But we were also best friends because while I sometimes wondered if he was interested in what I had to say, Alfred would talk about almost anything in the world involving him no matter how embarrassing it was to him. He was the first to admit that he was jerking off, back in seventh grade. If you asked him why he hated to play sports, he would tell you it was because he threw like a girl. Which he did, but what other kid would admit it?

For a while after he had gotten the Plymouth, Alfred would

15

pull up in front of my house every day, after dinner. "Let's ride," he would say, like Steve McQueen, whom we watched every Wednesday night on "Wanted: Dead or Alive." I would hop in the front seat and we would spend an hour talking as he took the car around town or squealing around the back roads behind the Woodmere golf course or out on Rockaway Turnpike, where we would park on a shoulder and watch the jets come roaring overhead before touching down at Idlewild.

Now I stood up, pushing open the screen door, and this time I said, "Let's ride."

We did, out toward the airport for about a mile. Then Alfred pulled off onto the dirt shoulder and shoved his gear shift up into neutral.

The airport runways were across the road to our left. To our right were empty lots and garbage dumps and acres of tall, waving sand grass about six feet high; in eighth grade Alfred and I would ride out here on our bikes, pick the grass, flake off the outside of the stalks, and cut them into golden peashooters. Now, parked along the road ahead and behind us were other cars. They belonged to families who were clustered around them, passing binoculars back and forth, craning their necks upward, watching DC-8s and 707s.

It was a good night for planes. The first one appeared as a smudge with landing lights, tiny in the west against the sunset. We could hear it, faintly. It got closer and bigger and the whine became a scream until we could see the blue and white PAN AMERICAN lettering and then, fifty feet above us, the plane passing slowly overhead and across the road toward the runways.

16

"Wow!" Alfred said.

Already another was visible.

"We should get a camera," he said.

"WHAT?" I yelled, over the screaming engines.

"WE SHOULD GET A CAMERA."

I nodded. I was trying to be friendly. The problem was I was angry with him, and after a minute I could figure out why.

It was that he had come over for the first time in a month, and was acting like there was nothing at all unusual. If he wanted something, why didn't he have the guts to ask?

"You try out for that team? Whatchamacallit?" he asked.

"_____"

"What?"

"I MADE IT."

"GREAT. That's great. Listen, I got an idea for you. You know Ellie Stern. Why don't you ask her to play tennis? Or we could play doubles. You and her. Me and Barb."

My legs were suddenly weak and I felt like someone had grabbed my stomach and squeezed it in one giant fist. Alfred was looking away, embarrassed.

"Is this Barb's idea?" I asked. Barb played tennis. That is, she had a father who gave her lessons and she spent half her summers at the junior high playing on the courts or banging balls endlessly against one of the cement walls that passed for handball courts.

"Well, yeah. I mean, we talked about it."

"Tell her to forget it."

"Why? She likes you. We want to do more things with you, and three people is awkward. You gotta find a girl friend."

17

"Oh. Is that right?"

"You want to. *You* know you want to. *I* know you want to. Anybody sees all those copies of *Dude* lying around knows you want to."

"How'd you know about them?"

"The time you were taking a shower and I was in your bedroom." Alfred grinned like he'd just pulled a fast one. "They were under the bed but sticking out. Boy, that's a good magazine."

"Alf, you were looking—" A big United 707 slid over us. I was so upset I hadn't noticed. "YOU LOOKED AT MY MAGAZINES. SOME THINGS ARE PRIVATE, YOU KNOW."

"Since when do you get pissed when I look at your magazines? Look, I'm only trying to help."

He actually sounded hurt. I could see he was right. Suddenly I was ashamed of myself for scolding him. At moments like this I wished I were alone with a soccer ball, juggling, with nothing more complicated on my mind than keeping a ball in the air.

"I know," I said. "Don't worry, Alf. I'm no faggot. Just, I have to do it when I'm ready."

"You don't know about life until you go with a woman," he said.

Such pomposity! Obviously he had heard it someplace and thought it sounded sophisticated. I felt superior enough to melt whatever anger I had left.

"There's all kinds of life," I said, looking out the window for more planes. And suddenly I saw a graceful way to change the subject. "Soccer is life too, you know. You should see these guys on Maccabiah. You never *met* guys like that."

18

4

It was true. They were the kind of Jews I hadn't met before. They were poor; most of them had emigrated after World War II. They worked as mechanics or janitors and lived in boxlike apartments in Hempstead or Queens and drove to practice in dented, postwar Fords.

There was Rabinowitz, *Hyman* Rabinowitz, the goalie, a forty-year-old machinist who had a concentration camp number on his forearm and never said a word during games. There was Abe Shaw, formerly Schonfeld, a halfback, who had fought with Irgun during the 1948 war; he told the most amazing stories about Arab women. There was Lou Marshak, janitor at a yeshiva in Far Rockaway, who even at first stood out as a silent, glowering man who never said much but for some reason seemed unusually well liked by the older men. He was forty, and when he sat down on a bench before showering—on one of the rare afternoons we played at a stadium with locker rooms—a roll of fat fell over his jock.

There were Stein and Bruch, who worked together in a gas station; they showed up for practice with a ball black from having been kicked around during lunch hours on the greasy garage floor. World War II had left Stein, whose family had come over from Poland in the 1930s, with a particular burden. Every few weeks he would punch some Greek or Irish fullback, get thrown out of the game, and trot to the sidelines, grinning unrepentantly.

19

"Dey tink Jews is faggots," he would say, still breathing hard. "Dey tink Jews iss chickenshit. Vell, dey *wrong*."

There was also Shimon Lupowitz, the center halfback. The other players called him Lupo. He was the oldest player on the team at forty-four. He worked nights as a janitor at a synagogue; by day he was a lift truck mechanic; he had hair all over his back, arms, and fingers, ropes for veins, and bricks for muscles. It was he who had cut off that first pass to me during tryout.

Was it coincidence that just as my father rejected soccer I began to idolize these immigrants, poor and from Eastern Europe but Jews who had survived concentration camps and suffering referred to in Temple regularly as "unimaginable" by our rabbi?

These men had suffered—and triumphed. They had fought to survive. They had wives or parents who had been turned into skulls and lampshades, and now they were strangers in a land of *goyim,* of bozos who thought that talking with a Yiddish accent meant you were some uneducated shyster, a character in the kind of jokes Myron Cohen told on *The Ed Sullivan Show.* I wanted to show them that here was somebody who listened to Elvis Presley and didn't know Yiddish but could sing *"Dayanu"* in Temple and maybe didn't fast on Yom Kippur but meant to.

After practice, Marshak, Lupo, a left inside named Sirulnick, and a few of the others would drive their battered Fords to Segal's, a bar owned by another Jewish immigrant. There they would rehash practice until they could no longer put off going home. I wished I could go to Segal's with them. I pictured us talking, first about soccer but then about the whole problem of being a Jew in Russia *or* Germany.

The only trouble was, they didn't seem to want me. The

starting team had been together for years. They partied together, drank together, and spoke to me like I was a Garden City Episcopalian, especially when they found out where I lived.

"Cedarhurst," Stein said, the first day Gatch brought me around. "Hotsy-totsy."

It turned out that his gas station—"service station," he called it—was in Lawrence, where he and Shaw resented their customers a little like my parents resented some rich cousins. He told me a number of stories about kids I knew, most of them stories about kids who had smashed a fender or a door and come in to have it fixed, peeling off huge bills to pay for it and tipping the mechanics on the condition that they kept it secret from their parents. He told them in a dour way, not trying to make it seem like there was anything charming in such behavior, and in case I had any illusions that they didn't associate me with my friends, Marshak set me straight about a month into the summer.

It was a weekday in June. The bank tower sign a few blocks from the field read 103 degrees. Players were going after the ball at a walk and making jokes about going to Segal's for beers afterward ("Hey! Hey, Lupo! Hey, you thirsty?").

Gatch blew the whistle to end practice. I went up to Marshak; he was sitting on the grass with Stein, Bruch, and Sirulnick. They were changing from cleats to sandals.

"Segal's. What street is that on again?"

Marshak looked up and shot an amazed glance at the others. Then he laughed. "Berger," he said. "Ven you *play* viz us, den you *drink* viz us."

I spent the summer of 1960 being tolerated: coming to practice, dressing for games, then sitting on the sidelines.

21

"Pain in the ass, isn't it?" Alfred asked one time. "Don't they even put you in when it's a slaughter?"

"No."

"Dumb. *Dumb*. I wouldn't take that shit."

"Don't be a jerk," I said. "I learn a lot watching."

○ ○ ○

And then it was April 1961. I was bigger, faster, stronger, I knew more, and I had gotten used to good players. When a pass came to me I knew how to move in and take it on the run. Instead of being panicked because I saw Stein bearing down on me, I could trap the ball, gauge his charge, and just as he jumped in on me, roll the ball away with the sole of my foot. Instead of thinking I had to get rid of the ball right away to the first free man I saw, I could hold on to it, screening the ball with my body, giving a couple of fakes to keep the defense off until I saw a man clear.

Meanwhile, Marshak had showed up ten pounds heavier even than the year before. After one practice he stood, hands on knees, bent over for a full minute. Then he lumbered over to the sidelines and threw up. Meanwhile, I controlled my own breathing and stood erect, making it clear that I wasn't winded at all, in case Gatch was watching me.

Still, for the first two games of the season Marshak was at wing. I sat on the bench in agony, watching him mishandle pass after pass. I sneaked a quick look at Gatch; he stood motionless, looking impassive, one hand fingering the whistle draped around his neck, the other shoved into the back pocket of his shorts.

One Saturday, the last week in April, we played Conquistadores, the Spanish team. The score was tied 2–2, a few minutes into the second half. I was too restless to sit on the

22

grass watching. I took a ball, went off a few paces, and began juggling to pass the time. Suddenly there were shouts from the few fans in the bleachers. A whistle blew. I looked up.

On the bleacher side of the field Lupo lay on the ground, curled up in a kind of fetal position, reaching one hand down to claw at his left ankle.

Gatch ran onto the field. He bent over Lupo, who was trying to sit up. Then he ran back toward the bench. "Berger. Get in there at wing. Marshak moves to halfback."

Marshak and Sirulnick were helping Lupo up. Lupo took one step, then collapsed. They helped him up again. Standing on his right leg, he put an arm around each of their necks and let them support him while he hopped off the field.

I told the ref I was going in, told Marshak the same, and went to my position.

"Hi," I said to the Spanish halfback, Torres, who was scraping at the ground with his cleats, waiting for the whistle.

"Hey, kike," he said.

"Hey, kike. Hey, Jewboy," called one of the other Conquistadores, softly. "We gonna kick you ass."

"Sure," I muttered. A 724 on my verbal SATs and all I could say was *Sure!* Despite the April wind blowing in from the reservoir I could feel my face grow hot.

"Gonna kick you ass," Torres said.

The whistle blew. Shaw put the ball in play with a free kick to Gribetz, our halfback. Gribetz dribbled a few steps, faked a kick to right wing, then wheeled and sent a pass on the ground to me.

As I moved to the ball I could see one of their halfbacks move in, slightly in front of me. When I stopped and raised my foot he stopped too. Then I let the ball go by me, the oldest fake in the book, but I did it perfectly, turned and ran past him. I could see him trip, trying to change directions.

Torres came at me next. I faked. He spread his legs wide. I sent the ball through them, raced by him, and crossed the ball into the middle. Even though it was picked off, it was a good cross, hit solidly off my instep.

"Way to go, kid!" somebody called from the sidelines.

Torres ran by me, shouting at his fullback in Spanish, then turning to me. "Try that again," he said.

By rights I could have called him a spic or sworn at his mother. But I knew that he was embarrassed. I walked back to my position, looking at the ground as if this was how I played every day.

We won, 4–2. I didn't score and I didn't have any assists. But I touched the ball about fifteen times and only lost it once. When the whistle blew I jogged toward the sidelines, where Gatch was looking at me, smiling. Lupo was sitting on an aluminum chair, barefooted. His left ankle looked swollen and blue.

"Good job," Gatch said.

Lupo had never said anything nice to me. Now he gave me a wink like we were old friends. "You play like you got goddamn tiger in your tank."

Could Gatch possibly keep me out of the lineup any longer? And once I was starting, wouldn't that be only a beginning? Was there any limit to a boy who could take a year and crack one of the best amateur teams in the country?

Maybe I should have worried that the players gathered around Lupo, laughing and joking in Yiddish, which I didn't understand, helped him to the parking lot, then headed off to Segal's without inviting me. But I had my mother's white 1957 Chevy Bel Air. As I drove home, my thighs ached and I could feel a bruise on my shin where one of the Conquistadores had kicked me. Sweat rolled down my chest onto my shorts. It felt wonderful. When the breeze from the highway began to dry me, that felt wonderful, too.

"President Kennedy today denied reports he is contemplating back surgery," said the radio announcer. I jabbed the button. Silence. I turned into my street lost in a fantasy of diving headers, shots on the run, goalies sprawled on the turf, and insults brilliantly worded in Spanish.

Couldn't I be a pro?

When I got home, instead of going inside the house, I changed to sneakers and walked out to Central Avenue and down toward the Village. Usually I went across the street to George's Luncheonette. There I could stand by the magazine rack pretending to look at *Sport* magazine and, when nobody was looking, put a copy of *Dude* or *Gent* magazine under my shirt and walk out. This time, though, I decided to get an egg cream at the diner, four blocks away, which meant passing by a row of antique stores and Bessinger's Piano & Organ Store. As I did, I glanced through the window.

She was playing one of the pianos, what I learned later was called an "upright," painted white with gold trim. Directly below, a big sign hung with wire from the ceiling (GRADUATION GIFT? SAVE $ WITH A SOHMER!!). She saw me, stopped playing to wave, and that made me forget all about being a pro.

I pushed the door open. "Hi," I said.

Sandy Bessinger stopped playing and spun around on the stool. "Hi," she said.

5

She sat behind me in homeroom, a girl I had known for four years. She had fair skin with blond hair and wide cheekbones, and people who saw her thought she was Irish. She was in no school activities and not many people knew her well. But the thing everybody knew about her was that she played piano and just like me, she was "good."

Every day she put in three hours at the piano even before she sat down to dinner, and until she was fourteen her parents had schlepped her—Alfred's word—into the city to take lessons at the Mannes School. At least once a year we had some sort of talent show at Lawrence; Sandy would come out and play something by Bach or Mozart or a Chopin piece with big chords that would make her actually lift herself off the piano bench.

The year before, *Newsday* had run a feature on her.

"A talented girl," my mother had said, looking up from the paper, the day the article had appeared. "A wonder she's still at Lawrence." Actually Juilliard had admitted her, her junior year; she had insisted on graduating normally and would enter Juilliard in September.

In a way it put the kids off; nobody knew anything about classical. But I was a soccer player; I knew what it was like to be unappreciated. We had had some long talks after college boards class; I loved her looks; I loved the way she rippled through Chopin pieces at school assembly.

For two years Sandy had had a boyfriend—Gene Kleven,

26

a year ahead of us and a freshman at Syracuse, where he was recruited by both AEPi and Phi Ep and drove back and forth along the New York State Thruway in a green MG with a canvas roof. His father owned Kleven's, a steak and lobster restaurant good enough to have been written up in *House Beautiful* and the restaurant my father took us to when we were supposed to "eat quality."

Gene had played basketball for Lawrence. I liked him. He would say hello in the locker room even though he was a senior. He didn't flick his towel at you when you walked by, and during basketball season, when most of the players didn't even pretend to study, he would leave practice with a gold and blue looseleaf binder and four textbooks wedged between his hip and cupped palm. Sometimes he had given me a lift home in his MG.

Sandy rarely mentioned Gene to me. But one night I had seen *Sandra Kleven* written in script across the back of one of her notebooks, and once Alfred had pointed to her as she walked down the hall ahead of us.

"See her foot? That little ankle bracelet?"

I looked down: just above the black Capezio on one ankle was a little gold chain and what looked like some sort of charm.

"I see it."

"Kleven gave it to her. She told Barb once she wears it all the time. Even when she wears socks it's inside them. It's her secret way of"—he gave an exaggerated sigh and clasped his books to his chest—"keeping him close."

Later, in homeroom, I had a chance to look at it. Actually it was two hearts and a chain and clasp and it was on the inside of her stocking. She did wear it every day; for a while I would check it, then get annoyed with myself and wonder when it would stop occurring to me, and just when I thought it never would, I noticed it one day and realized I hadn't checked it for a week.

In a way, Gene Kleven had made it easier to talk to Sandy. Nothing had changed in the last year. If a girl showed she liked me I was annoyed; it meant I might have to ask her out. With Sandy I had no such worry. I could talk to her as if she were . . . a boy! And today that made it easy to walk into the store where I'd never been before, look behind her at the music set on the piano, and say "Mozart? Beethoven? The Shirelles?"

Sandy laughed. "Czerny," she said.

"Who?"

"Czerny. He wrote exercises. Other things, too. These are finger studies."

There was a woman standing by the counter looking at flutes. A girl who seemed to be her daughter had wandered off to look through the rack of pop music along one wall. As I came in, the mother called her back. "Alice, I'm *buy*ing this for *you,*" she said.

Sandy's mother stood behind the counter. I had met her after college boards classes a few times. The word was that she was okay, but that Mr. Bessinger was a failure; a slob; a man who had decided to live in the Five Towns, then opened and closed two bookstores and a gift shop in six years before hitting on the field that had "won" the family some prominence. Supposedly this store wasn't doing well either.

"You working here?"

"Sort of," Sandy said. "I can use this piano to practice on, why not? This way my dad can go make some calls. How're you?"

She had beautiful, white, straight teeth; also, she was wearing a sleeveless blouse. Standing over her, I could look down past surprisingly muscular arms, down the armholes, to the front of the crispest, whitest-looking bra anywhere outside the Bloomingdale's lingerie counter.

"Pretty good."

"You don't have soccer these days. Or do you?"

"Not for the school. I play for a team," I said. "Amateur. But good."

"I can believe it," she said.

"Why?"

"Well, just I hear you're very good."

A rush of warmth went up my back and neck. I had to force myself to speak.

"I'm pretty good," I said. "Anyways for an American."

"Americans aren't that good?"

"Not like in Europe. There, kids, all they *play* is soccer. Soccer in the summer. Soccer in the winter. Soccer with little balls made out of rags. Soccer on school teams. Every town has its own team. They got a World Cup? Where the best teams from every country play each other? Last time the U.S. didn't even make the finals, that's how crummy we are."

Her eyes seemed to be focused and she was nodding as I spoke. Suddenly I was afraid I was boring her.

"Play me something," I said.

For a second she looked like she was about to say no. There was enough time before she answered that I knew she wasn't happy about it. But then she said, "What would you like to hear?"

"Oh." I frantically ran through a list of composers I knew how to pronounce. "Show pan."

"You like Chopin?"

29

"I don't know any. I just know you play the stuff."

Sandy laughed. "I play other stuff, too," she said. "Ever listen to Roger Williams?"

"Sure."

"The way he plays 'Autumn Leaves'?"

"I got the *record*. Fact, I *played* it a million times."

Sandy looked at me as if she was weighing whether to tell me. Then she decided. "Listen to this," she said.

How can I even describe what she did? If it was soccer, I could talk about how she took the ball with her instep or did a chest trap and exactly what her body did to fake her way over a fullback's outstretched leg. With piano, all I know is that she swiveled around on her stool, looked at the keyboard for a second as if it were a pool of cold water and she were thinking of diving into it. Then her fingers were playing and her arms leaping up and down the keyboard so "Autumn Leaves" sounded just like the record. First she played the song. Then she started playing these rippling passages around it sounding like a waterfall, and by the end she was pounding out big thick chords that gave me goose bumps along my arms. When she finished she turned to see my face.

"I didn't know you could do that," I said.

"Actually, I'm just starting." The place was suddenly quiet. The mother and daughter had left.

"For that you come in here to practice?" her mother called from the cash register.

"Oh, Mother," Sandy said. She looked up at me. "She doesn't like it, me playing pop."

"I like it," I said. "I play that all the time, no kidding. On the record."

She was nervous. "I just started working on it."

30

"I thought you just played classical."

"Until last year, right. But I changed my mind."

"Why?"

"Because I'm not good enough to be Dame Myra Hess but I can damn sure play better arpeggios than some of these clowns. Roger *Will*iams. Liber*a*ce. Jeez."

"Come on. You're a genius. You're going to Juilliard."

"Howie, there's a hundred pianists going to Juilliard. *Two* hundred. A lot of them better than me."

I understood immediately. It was just like soccer, where kids thought I would be a pro because I made All-County, not realizing that any Sicilian with two legs could come over and make All-County in Nassau. I felt a little stupid.

Except that then her face brightened and she said, "You're the first person I played it for. Did you like it?" as if it was important to her for me to say it again.

"God. A lot." And I was about to ask her something further about it when the phone by the cash register rang. Sandy's mother picked it up.

"For you, San. Mike something. Deutsch."

Sandy made a face. "Teutsch," she said, then went to the phone.

"Yes," I could hear Sandy say. "Oh. Hi, Mike. Sure. Sure I do. From math class."

I pretended great absorption in a few music books stacked on the piano. Mike Teutsch was a skinny senior with wide hips, a small head, and an enormous briefcase full of math books which he took from the library and read during study hall.

"Yes. God, it was hard. What? *Guns of Navarone.* Sure. No, I'd like to see it."

Her mother was sorting receipts by the cash register, pick-

31

ing one up, studying it, then putting it into the right pile, looking like she was playing solitaire.

"Oh, I don't know. Well, not Thursday. Sure, Friday's fine. No, the eight. Terrif. Well, uh, see you then."

She hung up. "Mike Teutsch," she said, drawing her mouth a little to the side as if to say she knew I was listening.

Suddenly, before I had a chance to control myself, I shot a glance at her foot. The ankle above her brown Capezio was bare.

My heart started pounding. To say anything was to admit I'd been listening, but the store had been so quiet that couldn't be such a crime. I looked up and around to mask my reaction, then back at her.

"I thought you were seeing Gene," I said. "Gene Kleven."

Seeing! The sort of outdated euphemism my father might use!

She smiled, a trembling smile. "Oh," she said with a casual toss of her head even I could see was rehearsed. "Oh . . . you know how those things are."

6

"Call her," Alfred said that night on the phone. And Barb Olman, on the other extension, said, "You *got* to. Abso*lute*ly."

And this time, six months older than that afternoon when Alfred had brought up Ellie Stern, having had six months more to think things through, I didn't try to change the subject.

"Maybe I will," I said.

Partly because Sandy wasn't Alfred's suggestion, partly because of my contempt for Mike Teutsch—*he* could call and I couldn't?—I actually got myself to the phone. In fact, for a week I got to the phone a number of times each day. On the chunky, white memo pad where each night I noted the things to do the next day I would write: *CALL SANDY (today!!)*.

But each evening after dinner I would tell myself it was too early or that I had to go to the bathroom first or that I should first sit down and make up a list of things to talk about with her. Or I would give her a chance to finish eating, or do her geometry, or watch "I Love Lucy," or finish practicing piano. And somehow, each evening, it would suddenly be ten-thirty and too late and I would whip out the memo pad again and write: *CALL SANDY (without fail!!)*. The times I actually sat down by the telephone my heart started pounding and my throat constricted and there was nothing to do but get up again. After a few weeks I knew she must think I was a complete idiot, and one night, when I had written myself one more note, I sat looking at it for a few minutes, then took the sheet of memo paper and ripped it in half.

The next Monday, during sixth period, I walked into Yearbook Office and there was Sandy, sitting and writing at one of the desks.

It was the end of April. Everything was winding up; talk was all about graduation, "senior slump," and colleges. In the morning, the yearbook staff had had to empty the office for a "final" organizational meeting of the Prom committee. As I left I had run into Donny Giarolomo, whose dropped *g*'s and black spit curl hanging down from the middle of his pompadour I sometimes tried to imitate, and

33

who had this week been named Prom chairman.

"Berger," he said. "Who you takin'?"

"To the Prom?"

"No. The inaugural ball. Course the Prom."

"I'm still thinkin'," I said and escaped to the lunchroom before he forced me to lie by pretending that—along with cheerleaders and beer parties—the Prom was beneath me.

"Guess who just joined Yearbook," Sandy said, now.

"You," I said.

"Right."

The yearbook was winding up, too. In a few days it would go to press. Sandy had come in to find famous song titles that would go underneath the pictures of each senior in the book.

"Great. Great," I said. I sat down in a chair and pulled out my history notes.

But after a few minutes I realized that Sandy's pen hadn't touched paper at all. She was holding it between her thumb and index finger down near the tip, and letting it flutter back and forth while she stared at a stack of senior pictures in front of her.

"You stuck?"

"No. Well, sort of. They think I know music. Well, okay. But I don't know *songs.*"

"The way you do it is, you can't wait for the perfect title. You just have to think of one."

"That's my problem. Thinking of *one.*"

"Let me see." I got up, sat in the chair next to Sandy, and looked at the pictures she had in front of her. The first one was of Gloria Wondrofsky, a girl who had had polio and had spent four years lurching through the halls with braces on both legs. And then I thoroughly amazed myself.

" 'Tiptoe Through the Tulips,' " I said.

For one horrible second I thought I had shocked her.

But then she smiled. "Maybe," she said. "Or how about this?" The smile became a grin. " 'Em*brace*able You.' "

Within thirty seconds Mr. Cohen was charging in from study hall saying, "Hey! You people in here are supposed to be responsible. Stop laughing. Berger. Get off the *floor.*"

After he left I looked at Sandy. She was still laughing. She would look at me and break into a little snort and stop. Then she would look at Gloria's picture and laugh again.

7

She still liked me! After that I made a point of spending sixth period in Yearbook Office every day. We didn't even have to speak. Somehow it made me happy just to see her smile at me when I came in and to be able to work on Yearbook galleys or even the Congressional Digest summaries we had to do for American history, knowing she was at work finding song titles at the next desk.

When the bell rang I would race down the hall to class, looking over the crowd, trying to spot her. If I got a glimpse of her blond hair or one of the white blouses she loved to wear, my heart would leap. I knew her locker: 3765444. It embarrassed me—did she know mine?—but I routed myself past it every time I was on the first floor.

Meanwhile, college acceptances came in. Alfred got into Cornell. I got into Cornell but hadn't heard from St. Louis. When I mentioned this at the dinner table one night, my father surprised me by saying, "You think you can get money out of zem?"

"Can I go if I do?"

He laughed. "Vell, let's say I'm curious," he said. "I figured out last night vat zis cost. Twenty tousand. At least."

"That's a lot," I said, trying to sound shocked, and never mentioned it to him again, afraid he might change his mind.

The team still didn't like me. I noticed it right away at the first practice after Lupo's injury. Gatch called us to the sidelines and, with Lupo standing there in street clothes, an Ace bandage on his ankle, made a little speech about my "fine" play the week before and how I would be starting at wing until Lupo's ankle was better, and then we went out onto the field, where I didn't get a pass for fifteen minutes.

At first I thought I was doing something wrong. We were playing nine on a side, not eleven, which meant I was covering a big territory. This meant I should get the ball more often, but every time the halfbacks had time to choose, they sent the ball up the middle, then out to Bruch at right wing. They just didn't want me in the play.

Nobody said anything during the scrimmage. I came off the field angry and sat on the grass to take off my cleats.

"It's gonna take a vile."

I looked up. It was Lupo.

"You mean before I get used to playing? I'm used to it right now."

"I mean before dey ged used to you."

"Nobody passed to me. What is this? They know I can play."

"They know you ken play. They don't know if they vant you to play. Frankly."

I stood up. Lupo was the biggest man on the team but also the mildest. I had never talked much to him. It seemed strange to see him out of uniform, dressed in tan, baggy slacks and a madras short-sleeved shirt. He wore a black yarmulka, which he didn't wear during practice. That surprised me, too; there was a lot of talk about Israel in the group and a lot of Yiddish, and one year we had forfeited a game scheduled for Saturday, but there was very little talk of religion.

"Why?"

"I don't know. Vell, yes I do. It's because you a rich kid from the Five Towns viz a new Chevy viz red seats and probably a girl friend every veek, and after practice and a couple beers at Segal's dese guys go back to crummy apartments in Hempstead viz no air-conditioning, that's vy."

He wasn't angry; in fact, he said it with a slight smile, this older observer of the human condition, then walked away, limping slightly and leaving me a little stunned. I wanted to race after him to explore the whole situation, except he had walked up to Sirulnick and there was no graceful way.

Well, of course! Wasn't it naïve of me to expect any different? In fact, wasn't it more of a threat that I was getting better? Wasn't that more reason for them to dislike me? But even then I felt there was something pat about his explanation. The team had players who weren't poor. On the second team, a mixture of men who never played and rarely showed for games, was an American-born doctor whose Corvette was certainly nicer than the Bel Air. But they talked to him; Shaw called him "Doc."

o   o   o

A week later, during morning homeroom, the principal announced that after school the French Club was sponsoring a performance of French music played by Sandra Bessinger, senior and "concert artist."

37

I whipped my head around. Sandy's eyes met mine. She shrugged.

"Can anyone come?" I asked when the bell rang.

"Sure."

"Good. Sounds interesting. What are you playing?"

"Oh, Couperin. Rameau."

"I never heard of them."

"Well, French Baroque composers. I told Miss Bronson I played them and she got all excited. It's about forty minutes' material."

"No 'Autumn Leaves'?"

She laughed. "Boy. I should."

"I *got* three Roger Williams albums, if you want to listen to them."

"I have all of them. Jeez, some of it is such junk."

As much as I wanted to like everything she said and did, I was annoyed. There was an arrogance about calling somebody else's favorite music "junk." We threaded our way down the hall, past slamming lockers and kids shouting. I didn't know what to say. And I wasn't much happier when she realized what she had done and looked sideways at me. "I don't mean it *sounds* terrible. But the *chords*. C, F, G. C, F, G, C. It's theory for four-year-olds."

She sounded so sure of herself I felt rebuffed. I almost decided not to go to the concert. And when I walked down to the little theater that afternoon—I had given my word, after all—I wanted to turn around and leave. There were three hundred seats in the little theater but not even ten kids, not counting two teachers and a very embarrassed Miss Bronson, who kept looking to the door as if expecting a flood of music lovers. Bonnie Landers and Sharon Kriss, friends of Sandy's, sat up front, but most of the kids were scattered, kids like the Peskin twins, who were in French Club because Miss Bronson gave a five-point bonus for joining up. Marty's arms were folded. Mort was making a paper airplane.

To give a concert and have nobody show up! At least somebody should stay to show her . . . what? That even if we didn't care about Chopin we cared about *her*! I took a seat in the second row.

Sandy didn't seem to be bothered. She stood up, looked around, and said, "Well, might as well do it. C'mon, guys. Mort. Marty. Sit down here. Make me feel like I got a crowd."

When they didn't move, she just stood there where somebody else would have looked paralyzed at Miss Bronson for help until they moved.

She played for about forty-five minutes, stopping before each piece to tell us a little about the composer. The pieces she played were short; most of them were fast.

She didn't win everybody over. Even to me she looked a little affected: the way she sat motionless, looking at the keys for five seconds before putting her hands on them to play; the way she hunched over, her face only inches from the keyboard, during slow parts.

At one point there was a snicker; Mort Peskin had his hand over his mouth. His brother was grinning. But most of the kids were quiet and respectful. They applauded when Sandy was done, and she smiled so graciously and with such poise that it frightened me.

This was a girl who didn't need anybody. I got up after the last number and headed up the aisle toward the door.

She came after me. "Howie. Wait."

When I turned, her forehead was furrowed in a way that didn't belong to a girl who needed nobody.

"I wanted to thank you for coming."

39

"No problem. You were good."

"I mean it. You don't know what it's like, looking around for all your friends and nobody shows up."

"Except the Peskins."

She didn't laugh and she didn't say anything. Instead she swallowed a few times and nodded. Finally, when the silence became too long to be anything else, I realized she was holding back tears.

"The Peskins," she said. She shook her head.

"They bothered you? Those jerks?"

"Well"—and now her voice was soft, without a trace of arrogance at all—"just I spend fourteen years of my life doing this. And everybody here laughs at it. Thinks I'm this weird kind of highbrow. They don't *respect* me."

If I'd been more confident of myself I would have kissed her. Instead, I reached out and put a hand on her shoulder.

"Hey," I said. "Hey, you were great."

She smiled. And at that moment I fell in love.

8

"I want you to help me out," I said. "Find out if Sandy would go to the Prom with me."

We were parked on the turnpike again, me and Alfred, watching planes. As soon as I said it, I knew something had changed. Alfred shot a look at me.

"Sandy. Bessinger?"

"Yes. Sandy Bessinger. I'm serious, Alf, you gotta help me. Find out if she'll go. If she *wants* to go. Then let's double. Me and you, her and Barb. That would make things a whole lot easier because I don't know shit about the Prom. I mean, do I need a new suit? Do I buy her a flower?"

"_____"

This one was Air France, a red and white 707.

"WHAT?"

"I SAID, WHY DON'T YOU ASK MICHELE BAUMGARTNER?"

"What's wrong with Sandy?"

"Nothing."

"I like her. I like her a lot."

Alfred was nodding. "Michele loves your ass. One date with her, ONE DATE WITH HER, BARE CUNT *AND* A HAND JOB. MINIMUM!"

"I DON'T LIKE MICHELE! I LIKE SANDY. JUST, THIS IS THE FIRST TIME I'M ASKING ANYBODY OUT AND YOU CAN MAKE IT EASIER FOR ME. JUST FIND OUT WHAT SHE'LL SAY. IS THAT TOO MUCH TO ASK?"

Alfred looked at me as if he were trying to weigh something very important. Then he leaned away from me, against the door of the Plymouth, putting his arm out of the window and playing with the rearview mirror. He pretended to be absorbed in the next plane, growing larger out of the west.

Suddenly I was furious. "What's going on here? I thought you wanted me to ask her out."

He shook his head. "_____"

"WHAT?"

"LET ME CHECK. I HEARD SHE'S GOING WITH KLEVEN AGAIN."

o   o   o

He dropped me back at the house. I walked around the block for a while. Then, still in soccer shorts and the sneakers

41

I had changed into after practice, I went down Central Avenue to George's.

I had miscalculated. In my stupidity and ignorance I had taken an innocent thank-you and a friendly laugh for something more.

Well, why not ask somebody else? Maybe not Michele, but Ellie Stern? Except, as I stood in front of the magazine rack pretending to look at *Sports Illustrated,* then picking up the new issue of *Dude,* I knew I wouldn't. If I could, I would be at a phone instead of trying to forget my anger by flipping through pages of airbrushed blondes with pink nipples, sitting on beaches or enormous heart-shaped beds.

"Okay, Berger. This ain't a goddamn library."

There was a burst of laughter that sounded like three machine guns. I jerked around to see five kids from school sitting at the counter, two of them girls. George, actually George, Jr., was wiping his hands on a dirty white apron and laughing. He was about twenty-five, fat, with a red face and pimples.

"Keep that hand out of your pocket," he said, shooting the girls a glance.

"George, you asshole," I said. My face was hot and I could feel a little trickle of sweat start underneath my armpit and run down my rib cage. I replaced *Dude* on the rack and went out the door, turning toward home, hating myself.

As I pushed through the screen door and came into the living room, the phone rang.

My mother picked it up. "He just came in," I heard her say. "Howie. *Howie?*"

"I'm home."

"For you. A girl."

"Who's that?" my father said. He was standing in the living room by the bookshelves, running his finger along the spines of a complete set of *American Heritage.*

"I don't know." I went to the phone in the television room. "Hello?"

"Uh, Howie?"

"Yes."

"Sandy. Sandy Bessinger?"

"Oh. Hi."

"How are you?"

"Fine. How are you?"

"Fine."

"That's good."

There was a silence. Then—no small talk, no nothing—but in a weak voice with a quaver even I knew appeared only when you like somebody a lot—she said, "Listen. The, uh, the Prom is in three weeks? Would you go with me?"

9

My father was standing just outside the room; his shadow fell across the floor. From it I could see he had stood up and was absolutely still. I kicked the door shut with my foot.

"Did Alfred just talk to you?"

"About what?" Sandy said.

"I was just getting ready to ask you," I said, then flushed, sure she wouldn't believe me. "To the Prom."

"Yes, well. I figured why should boys be the only ones asking. This is a new age. You don't mind, do you?"

Actually I had room to feel—just slightly—embarrassed

that I hadn't done it myself. "Oh no," I said. "I'm glad you did."

We hung up. I floated into the dining room; my parents had already eaten, but there was pot roast in a Pyrex dish on the stove. My mother stood by the counter, ripping off sheets from the box of waxed paper sitting on top of the refrigerator. My father came in from the living room. "Who was that?"

I realized I didn't want to say. To be casual about it ("Some girl. I'm taking her to the Prom") wouldn't have fooled him. Acting excited would have pleased them but would have embarrassed me.

"Something about school," I said.

Usually when I was late for dinner my mother was annoyed, shoveling food onto my plate without a word, but this time she had reached into the oven and took out a plate of pot roast, ladled some potatoes and gravy over it from a boiler on the stove, and said, "I think it's still warm."

"Pot roast. Great."

"We ate already," my father said. He sounded gentle too, almost penitent.

And then, so casually that I knew they had been thinking about it all day and that there was bad news coming that no pot roast would make better, my mother said, "There's a letter for you. From St. Louis."

Suddenly my heart was pounding as hard as it had when I picked up the phone ten minutes before.

My father, standing, took the envelope from the letter tray on the kitchen table and passed it over to me. I didn't want to open it. I held it to the light as if keeping the envelope sealed gave me the option to change the text.

"Open it," my father said. He had a cup of fruit salad in his hand and sat down at the table with it.

44

"I'm scared."

"They'll take you," he said. "You got boards good enough. The question is the scholarship."

"I should get one," I said.

"My guess is no," he said, which was his way of preparing me.

I ripped open the envelope. He was right.

Dear Mr. Berger:

St. Louis University is pleased to accept you as an entering freshman for its Fall term beginning Sept. 9, 1961.

Unfortunately, your request for scholarship aid has not been granted. While you were among many highly qualified . . .

I felt sick. I read it over twice and, with a mixture of embarrassment and anger, passed it over to my father. He read it without changing his expression, then laid it on the table. He looked relieved.

"Well, that's that," he said. "That's the verdict. Now you go to Cornell."

"Henry," my mother said.

"But I got in."

"Any idiot can get into a St. Louis University. The trick is gettink a scholarship, which you didn't do, which meanss I spend two tousand a year more for a vorse school, eight tousand in four years, so the answer is no."

"But they never give scholarships to New Yorkers."

"And next year you'll be a New Yorker. And the next year. And the next year. It's still eight tousand bucks."

"But when they see me play—"

"Howie, learn your limits. You're not even starting for

Maccabiah, except there's a man hurt. I could do zat. I could do zat right now."

"You couldn't play five minutes for Maccabiah. If you ever could."

"Howard!"

"Well, he couldn't."

"You don't talk that way to your father."

"Why not? He talks to me the way he wants. He doesn't know if I'm good or bad. The last time he saw me play I was a hundred forty pounds."

"He can talk any way he wants," my father said to my mother.

"Thank you."

"And I bring home the money, so who says how to spend it? Me. And I'm not sending eight tousand dollars to St. Louis, Missouri, period, the end."

It was a lot like arguments we had had before. But now there was the letter, still lying on the table as evidence that he might be right. Sure, Perkins didn't like to play New Yorkers. But if I was as good as I thought, wouldn't some word have reached him? Maybe my clippings were no more special than fifty others that had come into his office from Chicago or Los Angeles.

I ate in silence. My mother was putting some dishes away, shooting a glance at me now and then to see if I was upset. As, for a few minutes, I was.

But gradually I realized that I wasn't nearly as upset as I would have thought.

o o o

She had called me! What girl ever did that? Suddenly the pain of the letter faded. I wanted to tell Alfred—casually, of course, as if it were a piece of information I thought he might want to know, on a par, say, with answers to the trig homework. I forked the last hunks of pot roast and potato into my mouth, then raced up to my room.

And he was good enough to be excited. "*She* called *you?*" he said. "I guess I was wrong."

That freed me to be excited.

"I mean, would she ask me out to the Prom? A movie, maybe. But the Prom? Kleven would come down for the Prom."

"I guess she really likes you," he said.

Maybe I should have heard the reservation in his voice. But that night, for the first time in months, I spent most of the time before I fell asleep thinking not about soccer but about Sandy Bessinger.

I had practice the next afternoon. It was gray and cold for an afternoon in April as I pulled into the parking lot. There was the thumping sound of a ball being crossed. Sitting on the grass to lace my cleats, I stuck shin guards inside my knee socks, then stood and walked onto the field. Some of the men were in the field already, passing the ball around in a circle.

Sirulnick, who had a kid my age, turned and gave me a little wave with his finger. The rest of them saw me and noted it and went back to concentrating on the ball, moving casually as if saving energy.

One man, though, wasn't taking time, was jogging around the field, slowly, looking like he had to force himself. He was wearing cleats and shin guards in his socks, and as I watched, he stopped and started walking.

Suddenly I was so pleased with myself I stopped thinking about Sandy. This was Marshak, trying to get in shape, and that meant he was worried about me.

10

In the three games since Lupo's injury, I had started and played wing. Marshak had played center half and immediately one thing had become clear: he couldn't handle it.

It was one thing to play wing when you were forty-one years old and had to hide your gut by wearing your jersey outside your pants like a maternity dress. At wing, you could stand out by the sideline, making a few token moves to any ball that wasn't right at you. Or if the ball, God forbid, came at you, you could do a few stutter steps—as Americans called it, the immigrants not needing a name for the kind of fake they had absorbed into their feet when they were five years old—and send a cross floating into the middle and then take five minutes to catch your breath and get set for the next play.

But what about halfback, where you played offense *and* defense? Where one minute you were heading a ball out of your own penalty area and the next you were setting up plays seventy yards downfield? At halfback, Marshak was hurting the team.

In games, Bogen and Yagoda, our other halfbacks, knew Marshak wouldn't be covering his territory; I would see Yagoda, a little, skinny, hairy-legged man, younger than the other starters, cut into the middle from left half and yell for the ball; I'd turn to see Marshak, thirty yards out of position, breaking into a jog for a few futile steps, then coming to a stop, chest heaving, while Yagoda did his job for him.

48

The odd thing was, nobody complained. But when Lupo returned, Gatch would have to decide whether to put me back on the bench and move Marshak back to wing, or keep me at wing and bench Marshak. I was sure he wanted to play me. I could tell from the way he clapped me on the back after practice and from the way he came up to me after the game, exaggerating his smile to make up for the unfriendliness of the others.

"Good game," he said, after our game against the Vikings, a team made up partly from immigrants and partly from United Nations staff from the Scandinavian countries.

"Thank you."

"I mean it. You're getting better every game. *Every* game."

I was standing up, not even breathing hard after ninety minutes. Ten feet away, Marshak was lying on the grass, easing cleats off his feet.

He must have heard. After that game I saw him doing wind sprints, and when somebody asked him if he was going to Segal's he said no and made some crack in Yiddish about beer making him fat.

Let him try. Now I dribbled my own ball onto the field and, when nobody moved back to let me in, took it into the corner and juggled by myself.

Across the parking lot, Gatch got out of his car, reaching into the trunk of his car and pulling out a huge mesh bag of soccer balls. He threw it over his shoulder and walked like a short, swarthy Santa Claus across the pebbled concrete.

Usually he let us loosen up on our own, whistling us in only when he wanted to run us through a scrimmage. But now he blew the whistle right away. Most of the players stopped immediately and walked toward the goalposts. I flipped the ball into the air and ran over, lifting my knees high, keeping the ball up with my thighs.

Lupo, still dressed in street clothes, was standing with Gatch, a shoe on one foot, but a sandal and Ace bandage on the other.

Standing with him, also, was a young blond kid dressed in shorts and cleats, hands clasped behind his back. One of the practice balls was at the kid's feet and he was rolling it onto his instep and balancing it in the air, letting it curl around to the side of his shoe, then flipping it onto the instep of his other foot.

I figured he was a visitor. We had them sometimes: players from Chicago or Boston who were visiting relatives and wanted to work out.

"You still hurt?" I asked Lupo.

He nodded.

I turned to Gatch. "Does that mean I'm still starting this week?"

I asked politely because he was a grown-up, and my coach, after all. But I also asked for the pleasure of having him say yes.

Gatch looked at me as if deciding whether or not to deal with this now, then put his hand on my shoulder.

"Let's talk about that," he said.

11

Instead of telling me what he meant, Gatch looked up at the other players. "Sirulnick. Bruch. *Kumm a hier. Schneller.*"

"*Kummt,*" said one of the players. They were always telling

Gatch he spoke Yiddish like an American.

"What?"

"*Kummt.* You said *kumm.* It's *kummt.*"

"Ah, caught me again." Gatch smiled like a man who had done something so well no insult in the world could bother him. He turned the mesh bag upside down, dumping the balls onto the ground along with the red shirts worn during scrimmage by the second team. Then he reached into his Windbreaker, pulled out a folded piece of paper from his pocket, and shook it open.

"Couple announcements here," he said. "First place, the league board met last night, and we're proud to announce that this year the Nationals will be held in New York, which it hasn't been since 1954."

When he said the word *proud* he looked up and rolled his eyes to make sure we knew it was the league's word, not his. A few of the players laughed. Lupo snorted.

Maccabiah was in a Federation A league. There were A, B, and C divisions then for soccer leagues around the country. A teams were the best. The season ended in August; when it did, the A teams went into regional eliminations and the sixteen survivors met, usually in Chicago, for the Federation Nationals.

There weren't ten teams in the federation who could beat Maccabiah. The problem was, only the top team in each league qualified for the eliminations, and for the last three years we had finished second to Hercules, thanks mostly to their center forward, Miltiades Christofilakos. We called him "Milty." He was in his late thirties. Now he directed American operations for a Greek olive oil importer, but before that he had been the star of the Greek national team and had turned down pro offers from every big team in Europe.

He was tall for a Greek and very fast, and in our league he regularly scored two goals a game.

"It's not fair," I had told Alfred the year before, when he had spotted a *New York Times* picture of him. Milty had scored a goal in one of the quarter-final matches in Chicago. He was leaping in the air, feet curled under him, fist clenched, his beard almost as dark as his mustache.

"Why not?"

"Some dipshit Class A team in Miami wins *their* league and goes to Chicago. You think that's fair? Put us in Miami, we'd make it every year. *Every* year."

So it didn't matter much where the championship would be held. But now Gatch looked around again. He was still smiling.

"It's a championship," he said, "we have a very good chance to win."

We all looked at him dumbly.

"Vy's dot?" Gribetz asked, playing along.

"Because," he said, "Miltiades Christofilakos"—here he stopped, looking at Lupo as if they shared a secret joke, then back to the players—"is moving back to the holy land. His holy land. To Athens. He plays his last game next week."

In the explosion of laughter and cheers I was surprised to find myself laughing and shouting and shaking hands with Sirulnick.

"Let me finish," Gatch was saying. "Hey. Quiet down. *Sheket.* This means, this means we can win."

Win? This meant in three weeks when we played Hercules we might beat them for the first time in five years. It meant that I could be playing in a national championship at eighteen and maybe I wouldn't be the best player on the team but I wouldn't be the worst either and wasn't *that* something they would hear about in St. Louis?

Or at least that's how I would have felt except that just then Gatch moved in between Lupo and the blond kid and held his hand up for quiet.

"Here's something else," he said. "You know Lupo is hurt." He sent an open palm down toward Lupo's ankle. "And the last couple weeks we had a good game from young Berger. But, fellas, Lupo's going to be out another month, at *least* another month, and that's why we're very lucky today." Here he paused. He brought his hand up and let it fall on the kid's shoulder and nodded a few times as if he wasn't sure we could appreciate this unless we had some time to get set. "We have a new player. Joins us today. Yitzchak Osofsky."

Even with Gatch's hand on his shoulder the kid was playing with the ball. But when he heard his name he stopped and smiled. Then he made a short little bow from the neck.

"Yitzchak is not much for English," Gatch said, "being as he's five days off the plane out of Tel Aviv. He comes here with his mother, comes to America. Last year he was the star on the Israeli junior national team, and it is a pleasure to welcome him to Maccabiah. Yitzchak, shalom. Yitzchak will replace Lupo. Marshak moves back to wing. Howie goes back to second team."

I had guessed already. I knew from the way Gatch had avoided my eyes even when he mentioned my name. But what hurt was the applause and chorus of shaloms and fifteen men crowding around Yitzchak, smiling, firing questions in Yiddish, and shaking his hand because he was an immigrant like them.

53

"Doesn't he have to try out?" I said.

The laughter died away. Gatch looked at me. So did everyone else, including Yitzchak, who may not have understood English but could understand when fifteen people wanted to knock the block off a kid standing three feet away.

I was a little surprised myself. How could a kid whose finger trembled when he had to dial a girl's number talk up so freely to grown-ups? But I had always been that way and I wasn't sorry. I stood, one hand thrust into the elastic of my shorts, looking at Gatch.

"Usually. Sure," Gatch said. "But this is different, Howie. This boy is a top-notch player, here."

"Berger, go fuck yourself," Marshak said, pronouncing it *fock*.

Gatch wheeled around. "Marshak, shut up," he said. He turned back to me. It looked like he was weighing whether or not to say something kind. But then he stooped down and picked up one of the red shirts spread in a pile.

"It takes more than a few good games to start for this team, Howie." He tossed the red shirt at me. I caught it out of reflex. For a second I was tempted to fling it back at him.

But if I did that he might have thrown me off the team, and I wasn't ready to walk across the field to the parking lot knowing that behind my back everyone except for a puzzled Yitzchak was laughing at me.

I slipped the red shirt over my head. Walking over to the balls on the ground, I rolled one out of the pack and began juggling with it while Gatch assigned positions for the scrimmage.

He *was* good, Yitzchak. He got his passes off quickly. He trapped the ball close to him all the time and had a booming

54

header that could pick off a goal kick and send it forty yards downfield to his wing. Sometimes his passes looked wild, but after a while I saw that he was passing where players should be; our players, ten years over the hill, were out of position and making him look bad. Then, a half hour into the scrimmage, that stopped because Bruch, Stein, and Levy were pushing themselves to keep up with him, playing better than they had all year. But Marshak looked no better than ever.

Afterward Gatch came up and put his arm around my shoulder and walked me off a few steps away from the other players.

"Look," he said. "I didn't mean to be rough on you before. But do you see how they're playing?"

I could feel the sweat cold on my face and the wind cold on my thighs. "They played good," I said.

"With this boy we can beat Hercules. We could beat them *with* Milty. We could, not to jump the gun, but we could win in the Nationals."

"Maybe."

"Maybe. That's all we can expect out of life is a maybe. So don't get angry. And don't get angry that he's starting over you. He's good."

I was flattered. Probably because of my play the week before, he was talking to me like I was a grown-up. "Thing is," I said, "I don't compare myself to him. I'm comparing myself to Marshak. Marshak plays like . . . he's lousy. He's fat and out of shape. He's old."

If Gatch, ten years older than Marshak, was insulted, he didn't let me see it. He smiled. "Old?" he said.

"Relatively old."

"Look," Gatch said. "You're good. You're getting better.

But Marshak has been on this team eleven years. He was the best. Fast. Quick. Real quick, fake you out of your jock. You don't get rid of a man like that."

"If I'm better than Marshak I should play," I said.

"Well, you have been," he said. "But if he took two weeks and worked hard, I'm not so sure. He's not too old to get back in shape. You watch."

"I wish you would watch him. Him and me."

"Don't worry," Gatch said. "I'm watching."

And I think speaking up like that surprised him and made him reconsider. Over the next two weeks, whenever Marshak kicked the ball away or was late running to an open space, I would shoot a glance at Gatch. He stopped putting himself in scrimmage. He was standing on the sidelines watching Marshak as if trying to make up his mind. Marshak knew it, too. Once I saw the two of them from across the field, arguing. Gatch had his hands on his hips. Marshak was throwing his arms about.

But by that time I had something else to worry about.

What was technically known as "the Prom" took place in the Lawrence High School gym. There was dancing, punch and cookies, and a Prom Queen. The black and Italian kids stayed at the gym all night—anyway until midnight, when they left to go parking in the network of back roads along Reynolds Channel.

But to the Jewish kids, Prom Night meant renting tuxedos and buying formals and staying at the gym for only an hour before heading off to Manhattan for an all-night round of nightclubs. That made me very happy, because if I had had to dance I would have needed some delicate handling. I had learned to fox-trot if I had to, but the lindy was totally beyond me. And there were other intricacies of dating almost as confusing. So that night I called Alfred to get him to agree to double with me.

"I need you," I said. "I need you *and* Barb. You can tell me what corsage to buy. You can make conversation whenever it gets quiet. Alfred, I'm scared about this thing. No kidding."

"Well, that might be good. Yeah. Yeah, I could see how that would work out. Let me check with Barb."

"What's to check? You've been trying to fix me up all year. Don't you like Sandy?"

"Oh. Sandy's fine. Nothing wrong *with* Sandy."

"So what's the problem?"

"No problem. No problem. Tell you right now," he said. "We'll do it."

There was something guarded about his speech. It wasn't the way he talked at all. And why did he say nothing was wrong *with* Sandy? That sounded like she had a disease.

In the evening, to reassure myself and since I was still nervous about calling her, I found an excuse to walk by the store.

Sandy was there again, this time behind the counter. I pushed the door open.

"Howie!"

She looked so happy to see me, jumping off a stool and threading her way through pianos toward me, I was glad I had done it.

"You want to double with Alfred and Barb? I talked to him about it. He wants to."

"I like Barb. Alfred, him I don't know so well. But Barb is nice. Could we go someplace with a pianist?"

Immediately there was nothing in the world more worthwhile than finding a nightclub in the city with a pianist, and as luck would have it I had been studying *Cue* magazine all evening. "Basin Street East," I said. "Peter Nero."

"Peter Nero? Kind of cocktail piano?"

"Yeah, I think. He's on TV a lot," I said.

"Oh, great. This is going to be fun."

"Oh, hey. Hey, we'll have a great time," I said.

12

And hey. We did. All things considered.

I told Gatch I would miss the game on Sunday. He didn't mind as much as I hoped. We decided to take my mother's Chevy because it was newer than Alfred's Plymouth. It was a great relief. If Sandy and I sat in the backseat while Alfred drove, I might have had nothing to do but talk to her. This way I could pretend to be absorbed in traffic signs and exit ramps. I also had something to do with my hands.

On Prom Night, Alfred came over about eight. Wearing identical black tuxes, corsages in white boxes on the seats beside us, the two of us drove over to pick up "the girls." At Barb's house her father, a butcher with two stores, one in Lynbrook and one in Queens, stood us against the wall and made us wait through an endless succession of Polaroids ("Oh my. Oh, Doris. Looka this one!").

Sandy lived in one of the newer sections of Cedarhurst, on a street off Broadway ending in a cul-de-sac. The house was big, a bright yellow with a Cadillac at the curb and a black asphalt driveway curving around to a garage in back. The lawn was green, separated from the driveway by a row of large chunks—boulders, really—of mica.

Her mother came to the door, saying, "Hi, gang," but in a subdued way. While Sandy was getting ready, she seated herself at the piano, a skinny-faced woman with gray hair, and busied herself by looking through music books as if we weren't there. Mr. Bessinger never appeared. It was only when Sandy was putting her coat on that Mrs. Bessinger got up. She walked us out into the driveway, without smiling, to tell us how "lovely" we all looked.

But Sandy was smiling. We drove to the high school. As we walked across the darkened parking lot, waving to other couples, Barb said, "Oh, let's go!" to Alfred, took his hand, and hurried ahead. Sandy looked at me, and, smiling still, put her arm through mine.

The gym had been transformed. Strung from backboards and the ceiling was a blizzard of orange, red, and green crepe streamers. Signs (LHS SENIORS!!! . . . THE GREATEST!!!) covered the walls. A band was playing on a platform in front of the home-team bleachers, which were collapsed and pushed flat against the wall. As we came in through the big wooden doors opposite the cafeteria, the band started playing "Only You." Except for the crowd around the punch table, everybody was dancing. Angelo Martinelli, who never wore anything at school but black chinos, blue sneakers, and red socks, came by, still in red socks but wearing a tux. One arm was around Ginni Tuscano's waist, the other held her hand straight down toward the floor. He was crooning "Only You" in her ear.

"Want some punch?"

"Sure," Sandy said. She was wearing a sleeveless pink dress with a scoop neck and what looked like forty crinolines underneath. She had left her sweater in the car and there was a hint of cleavage above her gown. Her hair was parted in the middle and fell over her ears. She was wearing a pale pink lipstick and smelled of lilacs. The sleeveless dress emphasized her muscular arms, but I liked that too. Mrs. Schlicter, the art teacher, wore sleeveless dresses; when she slashed away at the blackboard her underarms wobbled and I had to look away.

The four of us pushed through the crowd to the punch table. Alfred downed his in a gulp ("Pineapple piss. Let's dance") and led Barb out onto the floor just as the singer finished his Tony Williams imitation and led the band into "Rock Around the Clock."

Now there was one moment of terror. I had decided to dance the slow dances. But *that* was a compromise. I felt almost as uncomfortable with them as I did the fast—I didn't know whether to place my hand on the small of a girl's back or wrap my arm around her waist and pull her toward me. But suddenly everybody seemed to be on the dance floor.

I hated them all: Alfred, who had deserted me; even Angie Martinelli, now scampering around the floor, legs flailing, showing flashes of red sock as he twirled Ginni around. I sipped punch from a paper cup. It was cold and sweet. I would have liked nothing better than to stand there, ladling punch into cup after cup while we looked over the floor and talked about college boards.

Finally the band went into "Twilight Time"—it was big on the Platters—and all around the gym boys moved in and clamped their arms around their girl friends' waists and looked serious.

"Good song," I said.

That was when I noticed Sandy was worried about something. She barely nodded.

"Wanna dance?"

"Sure. If I don't step on your toes."

I looked at her. Then it struck me: this was Sandy Bessinger, who was playing in Town Hall when she was four, liked Chopin and Bach, and might not even know who the Platters were!

"Would you rather not?" I said.

"This sounds funny for a girl," she said. "I hate to dance."

"Boy. Boy, you can't hate it as much as I do."

She brightened in a display of relief that made me see I had done her a favor.

"More," she said. "I don't even like the music."

∘ ∘ ∘

"Why did you call me anyways?"

We had been talking for twenty minutes, laughing about the way we had both been worried about dancing and how weird it was to see crepe paper in the gym and how dumb Angelo Martinelli looked with his red socks.

Sandy picked a few potato chips from a tray by the punch and smiled, a girl who wasn't afraid to admit she had done something incredibly brave. "Because I didn't know if you would call me."

"Well, you're right. Asking girls out makes me nervous," I said. "Maybe it shouldn't but it does. I wanted to call you lots of times this winter."

Sandy was still smiling. She ran the middle finger of her right hand under her bangs to sweep the blond hair off her forehead. "Well, it made me nervous calling you."

The drummer for the band began a pounding introduction and a big cheer went up. This song was "Chantilly Lace"; the singer was white but he had a deep voice and he was giving a good imitation of the Big Bopper, which everybody thought very funny, even the black kids who were dancing in the front of the gym, close to the band, points of light bouncing off their brilliantined hair. I saw Sandy flinch.

"You don't like any rock music?"

"That sounds like I'm a snob."

It did to me. But how could I be so crude as to resent anything about this girl who had just taken care of my biggest fear? "No. No. Not at all," I said. "It's a free country."

"Maybe I'm jealous," Sandy said. "I go home every day and I'm practicing till my wrists hurt. I mean they really *hurt.* But most kids think I'm weird. They think the music I play is weird."

"That's a lot like soccer. Kids here, all they know is *base*ball. *Foot*ball. *Bas*ketball. They don't know that everywhere else in the world kids never heard of Johnny Unitas. Never *heard* of him. But they heard of Pelé. They heard of Puskas and Stan Matthews."

And didn't her eyes light up as if I was confirming every nice thing she thought about me? Wasn't her head nodding up and down before I was halfway through with my little speech?

"That's the way it is in music," she said. "In Italy, people turn on their radios at work to hear opera. But I'll tell you one thing."

"What?"

"They heard of Roger Williams."

Who could be happier than me, driving the Chevy down over the potholes of Rockaway Turnpike to Grand Central Parkway, then through the Midtown Tunnel, the first time in my life I had driven to Manhattan?

To open the show, Peter Nero, playing a kind of cocktail-party background piano that made Sandy stop talking and look at him with the kind of eye I might give to a kid juggling in the street! Then Mort Sahl, with his brown sweater and rolled-up newspaper and jokes that made Alfred dart questioning looks at me so I could explain ("He's talking about when Eisenhower was president. *Golf.* Get it?"); and then the Limelighters, a folk trio whose jokes dazzled kids who had never heard comic routines that were both dirty and clever, and whose songs pleased even Sandy!

"You like them?" I asked, leaning over.

"Do I? I love them."

Afterward we walked the streets of Manhattan while bars closed, trying to sneak glances at beatniks, bearded, smoking pipes with God only *knew* what was in them; then we took the car back out to Point Lookout, where Alfred's parents had a summer house a block from the beach and where we were going to watch the sun rise. The sun was coming up by the time we were on Grand Central Parkway and by the time we were parking it was a bright yellow, but the water and sand glittered and we spread blankets and pretended to enjoy the view.

After a few minutes Alfred got to his feet, reached into the back pocket of his striped pants, and pulled out a key.

"We're going back to the house," he said.

"Hey. Great," Barb said, pretending she was surprised.

"We'll stay here," I said, looking at Sandy to get her nod.

A minute later, the two of them were tromping off through the sand, Barb holding her Capezios in one hand. Sandy and I were alone.

13

Could a girl say no when a guy had spent sixty dollars on her? Could a girl say no when she had seen Peter Nero and Mort Sahl and was still wearing the white corsage she had lifted tremblingly fresh from its box ten hours before?

Most of all, would this girl say no when she had made it plain in every way possible that she liked me? Oh, not to go all the way. But at least to kiss me back with something like the passion Natalie Wood had reserved for James Dean in *Rebel Without a Cause,* which I had seen seven times.

It was about two hours after high tide. Fifty feet down the slope the sand was wet and dark; where it changed, a long, irregular black line of tar, seaweed, and flotsam ran parallel to the water while a tractor tread and a motorcycle tread wove patterns higher up. Sea gulls were walking rapidly along.

About six blocks toward Long Beach, a tiny dot of a man was standing knee-deep in the water, casting. An even tinier dot sat on the sand nearby.

Sandy lay back on her elbows on the blanket. Her legs were stretched out straight and crossed at the ankle. There was no charm bracelet around her ankle. She looked tired, her eyes bloodshot from the night without sleep and the two gin and tonics a fake driver's license had earned her at Basin Street East.

The only surprise was that whereas all night she had been talking, laughing at my jokes, and looking at me, now she wasn't talking to me at all. But I was in no mood to look for omens.

"What are you going to do when we get home?"

"Sleep," she said.

"So am I."

"Don't you have games on Sunday?"

I didn't tell her that I wouldn't play even if I went. "This is the first I missed."

"Well, I didn't practice yesterday. That scares me."

"You got a concert or something?"

"No. Just, when I let a day go by that's three hours I can never get back when I could've been getting better. I'll make up for it tonight, but not all the way."

I picked that moment to put my hand on her shoulder and, when she turned to face me, checked to make sure we were alone, and kissed her.

She didn't resist. Not exactly. She even parted her lips a little, and when I put my tongue inside her mouth, she opened a little wider and let me inside.

But passion? She wasn't Natalie Wood—she wasn't even Alexandria Robinson—and when I put my arm around her she sat up. "Listen," she said, and from the way she was making herself look directly into my eyes, a little furrow creasing her forehead just above her nose, I knew there was trouble. "We have to talk about something. Did Alfred talk to you?"

"About what?"

"He didn't. Damn. Okay." She brought her knees up, hugged them, and rested her cheek on her knee, looking at me. "About that I've been going out with Gene again."

"I thought you broke up."

"We did. But not really. I mean, he wants to go with

other girls, but no, we still date. Maybe you think it's crazy, telling you this. I mean maybe we won't even go out again. Maybe you don't care. Who knows. But I want to go out with you, so I hope you do. Just, I want you to know the truth because, well, because I want you to know how things stand. For example, Gene's in town tonight. That's who I'm seeing tonight. I'm not practicing."

So that's what Alfred knew, I thought, in words. "I don't get it. Are you going steady?"

"No."

"So why tell me about Gene Kleven? I know about him."

"You know everything? How long we went out? How long we broke up?"

"You went out with him last year."

"Try the last two years. And we didn't break up. We still see each other. Just we see other people, too."

Something about the poised way she put things ("Try the last two years") made me angry. "See other people, huh. You mean *he* wanted to see other people. *He* wanted to, so *you* have to."

"Well, no—"

"That's what you said at first. He wanted to see other girls. So you needed somebody to show him you got a date. Well okay. Okay. You want to use me like that, I don't mind. But when you take my money, my *par*ents' money, and let me spend sixty bucks just so you can show fucking Gene *Klev*en up in Syracuse you don't need him, well, that's going too far, Sandy. That's just going *too* far."

She wasn't saying anything.

"That's really using people," I said.

To dramatize exactly how rotten it was and how disgusted I was, I heaved myself up and marched off, up the sand, my black Florsheims slogging through the dunes, through the beach wall, and toward the Chevy, which was parked on the road a block away.

How could she do it? How could she have convinced herself that telling me was a service? Suddenly, it was just like the moment on the dance floor: I hated Sandy, hated Alfred for leaving me feeling alone and ridiculous, while he was making out with Barb. I hated people who knew how to tip the maître d' at Basin Street East for the midnight show. I hated the hundreds of boys who knew that after the Prom they would park on the dirt road by the Channel if they were Italian and by the tennis courts if they were Jewish, boys whose dates would willingly part their legs for them and let them touch everywhere!

The only problem was that once I reached the car, I realized there was nothing I could do but stand there. Because if I left, the three of them would have no way to get home and wouldn't that story be all over homeroom by Monday morning?

The jacket felt hot against my back. I took it off and opened the trunk to lay it inside. And there, set inside the spare tire like an egg in an eggcup, was my soccer ball, crusts of mud still caked on from the last practice.

It looked like an old friend. Picking the ball out of the tire, I dropped it onto the instep of my loafers and began juggling. First one foot, then the other, then back and forth, and then I tried bringing it onto my thighs, but my pants were too tight and the ball hit my knee and bounced off. I ran after it, leather heels clattering over the pavement, and brought the ball back to try again.

Except when I turned, there was Sandy, standing by the Chevy. She was looking at me, curiously. At least, I thought it was curiously—it was the kind of expression you might get from someone looking at a monkey, though a very intelligent monkey.

"Hi," I said.

"Hi."

"Ever see me do this?"

"Play with a soccer ball?"

"Yeah."

"Howie, I—I don't want to see you play with a soccer ball."

"Oh no?"

"No. I want to tell you to stop being unfair. I didn't take your money. Or your parents' money. I called you up because I like you. I want to go out with you. This isn't fifty years ago. People don't have to go steady to go to the Prom. And you don't have to get mad because I told you the truth."

"I'm not mad."

"You are. And that's unfair."

"Why did you tell me?"

"Because I thought maybe Alfred did. I didn't want to spoil things. Just, when you kissed me I thought I better tell the truth."

"Big deal. I'm sorry I got you so scared. One kiss, you panic."

"It's not that I didn't want you to kiss me. I do. And I want you to ask me out, too."

"Why?"

"Because, for saying 'Good playing' when I played at the French Club."

"Oh."

"I needed that. And *other* things. For 'Tiptoe Through the Tulips' when I needed something for Gloria. And for

68

all the times we talked after college *boards. Lots* of reasons."

She wanted me to kiss her! She wanted me to reach over and put my hand on her breast and stroke those muscular arms and maybe reach up under that dress and under the crinolines to whatever mysterious things she had on underneath!

Well, if that was the case, maybe it wasn't so bad to have a rival. Wasn't it possible that if I took on Gene Kleven the way I could take on a halfback from Conquistadores, I could dribble by him, too? Wasn't it time to try?

"You going to see Gene all week?"

"Oh no. No. Just tomorrow. Tonight and tomorrow."

"Well, maybe Tuesday night maybe you want to go out. Like, just to the boardwalk."

She leaned forward, across the prow-like tail fins of the Chevy, her eyes bright.

"Yes. I do."

"Great. Hey, great," I said. For a second, I had an impulse to work with the ball again to show her how I could do it right. But then it seemed more natural to lean forward and kiss her. She kissed back, and if it wasn't with the passion of Natalie Wood, it was enough. Heart pounding, ready to learn a new kind of juggling, I flipped the ball into the air and bunted it with my knee into the spare and closed the trunk.

"Let's take a walk," I said.

Two

14

Out beyond the sand it was dark, though you could see the white of the breakers. Every few hundred yards there were bonfires on the beach. People had turned the wire litter baskets upside down, crowning piles of charcoal bricks; they would thrust in some newspapers, light the pile, and sit around on blankets toasting hot dogs and Campfire marshmallows. Stretching up the boardwalk were the game booths, little sheds of wood or plasterboard with flashing yellow, green, or red neon marquees. About ten blocks away a small roller coaster and a Ferris wheel rose in the night sky.

It was Tuesday, and all right, maybe the Long Beach boardwalk wasn't Coney Island. Wasn't every guy my age walking along the boardwalk holding some girl's ID-braceleted hand? This was a boardwalk I had been to each summer since I was twelve; Alfred and I knew every inch, which made it the perfect place for a first date. The only trouble was, walking up the concrete ramp at Lincoln Street, I realized I was scared stiff.

For three days I had tried to pretend that Gene Kleven didn't exist. It was much more satisfying to fantasize about the date: how we would walk along the boardwalk, laughing through Bingo games and slice after slice of pizza, steaming in the night air; we would kiss on the beach, then take a long drive in the Chevy, parking on some deserted road while Sandy unburdened to me the story of her lonely last year.

But Sunday afternoon I had actually seen Gene Kleven in town; at least, I had seen his green MG with the tan canvas top scooting down Central Avenue, and though I immediately turned away, my heart pounded and my legs grew weak until I looked again and made sure there was no one in it but the driver. Tonight, when I picked up Sandy, she had been dressed in bermudas and Capezios, looking cool and . . . sophisticated, not like someone who was lonely at all.

For all I knew she had been on the phone talking to Gene as I pulled into her driveway. Suddenly I was so nervous I could hardly speak as we drove out to Long Beach, and it hardly made things better that Sandy was clearly trying to relax me.

"I like this boardwalk," she said as we left the ramp and turned north, toward the game booths. "Definitely better than Playland. Here you can play games. Go out on the beach if you want. You're not always getting pushed around by the crowds. Want to play the basketball?"

"The" basketball meant a booth with three hoops set back behind racks of prizes. Sinking three in a row gave you your choice of a giant green panda or a Coke bottle with an elongated green neck and the lip pinched to give it the shape of a swan, or coupons which you could save all summer and redeem in September for transistor radios or eight-bladed Swiss camping knives.

I knew there was some witty story I could tell her about

coupons or basketball, but my mind seemed to have frozen. "Sure," I said.

I sank my three shots to win ten coupons. Two booths later, when she missed trying to knock over a pyramid of metal milk bottles with three baseballs, I hit two and won ten more.

"You're good at these things," Sandy said.

We bought cotton candy. Then we stopped at Steeplechase, which two summers before, Alfred and I had made our specialty. It consisted of a metal hill, painted to look like some English countryside, with eight gray metal horses fixed in eight slots leading uphill.

The players stood behind black levers. If you pressed your lever just right, a ball shot up out of a hole in a glass box a few feet away, went into another hole, and your horse moved up one notch. The first horse over the line set off a bell and set a neon WINNER sign flashing. I won three times in a row.

Sandy was giggling; when the bell rang for the third time she grabbed my shoulder.

"Whaddaya want?" the manager said, looking at me suspiciously. It was the manager from two years before, a short man with a greasy black pompadour and a blackened apron so full of dimes they clinked and jangled as he walked. "Wanna panda?"

"Coupons," I said.

He looked at me again. "I remember you. Usta come by all time."

"Not *all* the time," I said.

The fourth time I was beaten by a little kid with tortoise-shell glasses that hooked around his ears, being egged on by a group of friends all bigger than he, who pounded him on the back and shouted, "Way to go, Squirt," when his horse crossed the finish line.

By this time a little crowd had gathered. "Getting bored?" I asked Sandy.

"God, no."

"Good. Let me do one more."

The bell rang. I pushed the lever. The first ball swished through and I pushed it again, keeping my arm relaxed, trying to make each motion just like the motion before, not letting myself look sideways at the kid, afraid it would make me tense. The crowd was cheering for him; Sandy was yelling something at me. The horses moved up, exactly together until the end when my ball plopped through, the bell rang, and the WINNER began flashing.

"Are you good at every sport?" asked Sandy when we had left and were waiting at a pizza booth for two slices.

A rush of goose bumps went up my spine and neck. For a moment I wasn't worried about Gene Kleven. I felt drained and good, just like I did after a game. The pizza slices came and they actually were steaming. We folded them over so they wouldn't droop and walked out.

"A lot of them, actually," I said.

o o o

"Thing is," she was saying, "people don't respect it."

It was an hour later. She had been talking about playing the piano and how bizarre most of the kids thought it was.

"Do you hate rock 'n' roll?" I asked. "I mean really hate it?"

"Why?"

"Well, because one thing. Rock 'n' roll, that's what everybody likes. Maybe it's loud. Maybe it's even simple. I don't

76

know. But something like, well, like 'Roll Over Beethoven.' Remember that?"

"God. Yes," she said.

"Well, you may not like it. But couldn't you learn to play stuff like that? I mean, how long would it take? Then you could play both. And God, Sandy. Kids would *love* it."

"Me play Chuck Berry? Howie. Roger Williams stuff, sure. Or the guy we heard. Peter Nero. But Chuck *Berry*?"

"Or Jerry Lee Lewis. I know he's a clown. But couldn't you do all that stuff?"

"I don't know."

"Because if all it takes is learning 'Roll Over Beethoven' or 'Great Balls of Fire' so you play it at parties . . . Jeez. Think how funny it would be, you playing that stuff. Kids would *die*. Just *die*."

She actually appeared a little insulted. "So would my piano teacher," she said.

But after we'd walked on a few hundred feet, she said, "But maybe. I like Roger Williams."

I took that as a way of making me feel better. It worked. "Walk on the beach?" I asked her.

"Okay."

There was a limit to how many games you could play. There was a limit to how many times Sandy could tell me I was good and I could pretend that all I wanted to do with her was talk about music.

It was seventy degrees, but I started to tremble. It was all I could do to keep my voice steady as we walked down one of the ramps to the street, then walked under the board-walk and out onto the sand. We scuffled along through the sand, sneakers squeaking, until it was dark enough to see stars. The noise of the breakers was as loud as the barkers and calliope had been five minutes before. I stopped, pulled her toward me, and, trying to control my trembling arms, put my arms around her waist just like I had seen it done in a thousand Burt Lancaster movies.

Sandy moved close to me. I kissed her once, then again, parting my lips a little. Then I looked down at her and smiled. She smiled back.

"I'm glad you called me," I said. "About the Prom, I mean."

"So am I," she said.

I kissed her again. My eyes were open. My heart was pounding but the trembling had stopped. About ten yards away another couple lay on a blanket on the sand, legs wrapped around each other like braids. I moved my hands up Sandy's back, experimentally feeling the little edge of her bra strap. She reached up and kissed me again.

But when I moved my hand around to her breasts she stopped me. "Not here," she said.

"Where should we go?"

"I don't know. Just not here."

"Okay."

She sensed my disappointment. "We can try the tennis courts."

For a second that was terrifying enough to make me want to say no. Did Kleven take her there the year before? If so, what would the kids say, seeing us pull in ("Jeez. Sandy again. What's she got, anyhow?")?

But there was nowhere else to go. "Good idea," I said, as if I had cast my eye over all the options. "I like it."

When we pulled in, Sandy said, "Dim your lights," making clear she knew it must be my first time. We cruised along the dirt road, by a long line of cars parked on either shoulder, until we found a space against the wire fence behind the courts. I smiled at Sandy, but she was looking around through the windows. And then, five minutes after I slid across the front seat and put my arm around her, she stopped my hand because it was trying to unbutton the top button of her blouse.

"Do you, uh, not want my hand there?"

"I don't know."

"You don't *know*?"

"Well, I'm not sure. This is so soon."

Even I knew what a hackneyed line that was. "Sandy. If we *like* each other," I said.

She backed away a little toward her window. "Also, I keep thinking, I know it's dumb, but I keep thinking what if this is all he wants."

"What's all I want?"

"You know. My body."

"Oh. Jeez."

"I know. It isn't what a girl should think who lives in the Five Towns and listens to Jean Shepherd. But that's what I feel."

"Well. You've done it before."

It was as if I had hit her. She looked at me. She didn't say a word.

"You mean with Gene Kleven."

"Course Gene *Kleven*. What other Gene do you know?"

She looked at me incredulously. "God, Howie. We went out for months before I let him do *anything*."

Idiot! Jerkoff! To promise yourself not to think about him and then mention Kleven in a way that made all the pleasure drain out of her face!

"I know," I said. And immediately blushed because I didn't know at all.

"Well, I'm not sure you do. But it's true."

By now I didn't even trust myself to say a word. We sat, both of us, looking down at the brocaded seat cover, then out of our respective windows at the row of other cars. Some had parking lights on; some had their lights completely off. Occasionally you saw a head raise up to the window, then duck down. I wondered what she had done with Kleven, here or the other places he could have taken her.

And then I surprised myself because as I looked out my window I began to feel better. At least I was here! At least people could see the white Chevy and some of them would know it was Howie Berger! Two cars down was Marty Oestreich's gray Ford Fairlane. Maybe tomorrow he would come up to me in English class, punch me lightly on the arm the way he did with Stevie Braun, and say, "Hey. Hey, Berger. Get any last night?"

Besides, hadn't she just said she had held Kleven off for months? And maybe that was a silly, trivial thing to want to hear! At least it made me stop trembling so I could say, "I believe you. Anyway, it's none of my business."

I reached over and kissed her again. Sandy put her arms around me in almost a motherly way. For a while we kissed. I wondered about putting my tongue inside her mouth, but somehow it seemed easier to work on her blouse again. This time when I started unbuttoning the top button she even leaned away to make it easier. I put my hand inside and then inside her bra.

I'm really doing this, I thought. If she had touched me— if I could have touched myself—I would have come.

"I really like you," I said.

"I'm glad. Because I like you."

"I really do."

It was the first time I had ever said that to a girl. It amazed me I could say it that easily.

I was careful not to say more. But to see her smile when I said it! To see her reach a hand out and put it on my shoulder and feel the way she squeezed me! Suddenly I didn't care about bare tit at all. It was enough that she liked me! It was enough that she admired me ("Are you good at every sport?")! I put my arms around her again and kissed her. Now I did put my tongue inside her mouth; it felt almost alive, with a faint taste of pizza, and then she put her tongue in my mouth and the fact that she did made up for the fact that it felt exactly like a wet snake.

I put my hands on her shoulders. "This makes me hungry," I said.

"Carvel?" she said.

"Sure."

○　○　○

I wanted to see her the next night, but Alfred advised against it and luckily I had an excuse.

My mother had tickets to hear Isaac Bashevis Singer—she used all three names—at Congregation Sons of Israel, exactly the kind of evening I would have paid real money to avoid, but this time she was asking me to go.

I had never heard of him. But my mother had read Singer aloud in Yiddish to her mother in the thirties and wanted me to learn about "my heritage," and if I went there was no way in the world I could be tempted to call Sandy.

"Sure," I said. "I'll go."

"Just like that? Sure?" my mother said.

"I know. Will miracles never cease," I said.

15

I saw him as we came through the glass doors to the hallway where about fifty people, all adults, mostly women, were standing and talking. Actually, his back was to me; he was unstacking folding chairs from racks outside the library where, after Singer read, there would be a reception. As we came down the stairs I saw Lupo pick up chairs, holding them under each arm, and disappear into the room.

I was wearing my green suit with thin lapels, a thin green tie knotted tightly against my tab collar, black loafers, and white socks. But Lupo was wearing baggy blue janitor's pants and a blue shirt and yarmulka, limping badly as he brought each load of chairs inside.

Would he be humiliated seeing me? I felt affectionate, superior, angry. I turned away, hoping he didn't know I was there.

Halfway through the reading, though, which was in heavily accented English, Lupo came into the auditorium and took a seat in the back, listening intently.

Afterward, as we filed in to shake hands with an unsmiling Singer, nodding his bald head quickly to each woman, I saw Lupo carrying trays of honey cake in from a kitchen in back of the library and setting them on the tables.

"That's Shim Lupowitz," I said to my mother. "He's on the team."

"Do you want to say hello?"

"Yeah. Yeah, I should," I said.

Only at that moment, Lupo picked up a tray of glass punch pitchers, some empty, some half empty, and some stacks of plastic tumblers, stacked one on top of the other. Wheeling toward the kitchen; he stopped short to avoid Gloria Wertheimer's mother, who was racing toward the bar, and the pitchers and glasses slid off the tray.

He grabbed for them with his free hand. But the crash was deafening. Red punch splashed up and spilled onto the floor. Women leaped back and there was suddenly a complete silence.

Lupo stood looking down at the broken pitchers, the puddles of Hawaiian Punch and ice cubes. Plastic glasses were still rolling around the floor.

"Oh, Jesus *Christ*," Mrs. Wertheimer said.

Singer was looking on as if wondering whether this were the moment he should leave without being noticed.

"I don't think so," I said to my mother.

○   ○   ○

The next day we played Conquistadores. It was Thursday. Usually on weekdays there were more people on the field than in the stands, but Conquistadores always drew a crowd—Sirulnick maintained it was because so many Mexicans were out of work—and the bleachers were about half full.

Before the starting teams trotted onto the field, Gatch came over from a conversation with the ref and two men I recognized as being league officials. He headed straight for me and put his hand on my shoulder. "Got a favor," he said.

"Okay."

"Well, maybe you'll like it. They want a juggling contest half time. Something for the crowd. Will you do it?"

And though I'd come to the game angry and humiliated that I'd be on the bench, I was flattered too. Juggling contests were popular with crowds but I had never been in one before.

"Sure," I said.

"Good. Wonderful."

As soon as he left, I was angry with myself for being so cooperative. When the whistle blew I sat by myself, on the grass, watching Stein nudge the ball over to Bogen, him passing back to Goldstein while Marshak moved out a few tentative steps beyond the midfield. I hoped he would trip. I hoped he would get kicked. I hoped he would have the ball with the goalie out of position and nobody on him and kick the ball into Peninsula Boulevard so everybody could see he no longer belonged on the field.

But by halftime I had completely forgotten to be angry. We were winning, 3–1. A few minutes before the half I took a ball and began warming up, just trying to keep the ball in the air, nothing fancy. There was a minute after the halftime buzzer while the teams came off, grabbing orange slices, collapsing onto the grass around Gatch. Then one of the league officials came out onto the grass in front of the bleachers and announced the contest.

"You're on," Gatch said to me.

It was three of us against three of them. Our other two were Bruch and Stein. Two of the Mexicans I didn't recognize. The third was Torres, who didn't seem to recognize me. We stood in a row, about five yards apart, a ball at our feet, me the only one with a clean uniform. The crowd was quiet. Somebody called out something in Spanish. A hundred "Shhhhhh's." Then the referee called *"Go!"* and with a flip of the instep we were off. And right from the first I was sure I would win.

Maybe it was that the ball happened to roll so neatly onto my foot and that the flip into the air was exactly the height that I wanted. The ball hardly spun at all. For the first fifteen times I just kept the ball on my left instep. Then I switched it to the right; it was my weak foot, but years of practice had made it strong. The ball kept coming off my instep, never higher than three feet off the ground. I could see clearly the smudge marks on the white panels, little cracks in the black, the faded red of the FIFA stamp.

There was a gasp and I knew someone had missed. I brought the ball up to my thighs. Did I dare to look away? No, I didn't. Get it out of my head.

Fight myself. Fight the temptation to give my right foot equal time with my left. Fight the temptation to juggle faster than I had been doing.

"Shit."

That was Bruch. Again there was a little murmur from the fans.

I could see the grass, brown and green, around my feet. Out of the corner of my eye I could see one of the Conquistadores still juggling; I knew it was him from the green pants. When I brought the ball up to my thighs I could see the players, standing by the sidelines, arms folded, watching, and beyond them the crowd.

Then, almost at the same moment, Stein missed, and so did one of the Mexicans.

Careful. I brought the ball down to my left instep and let it hit off there again; it was unimaginative but safe. And then out of the corner of my eye I saw the ball hit a brown knee and bound away, and then there was a cheer, some clapping, and whistles. For good measure I kept the ball in the air another few seconds, cradled it on my instep, and flipped it up into my hands.

The ref came running over, a tall Englishman who had

just retired from playing last year. He had done some of our games: he was always on top of the play, showing how fit he was; halftime, he usually liked to take the ball and shoot on goal himself. "The winner . . . from Maccabiah. . . . *What's the name, young man?*"

I told him.

"HOWARD BERGER."

More applause. If nobody crowded around me, at least some of the Maccabians were cheering as I came to the sidelines. Stein and Bruch were applauding, smiling, to show they didn't take it too seriously. But Gatch came over, and from the gentle way he cuffed me on the forehead, I knew he was pleased. "I knew you could do it," he said.

It wasn't until they were ten minutes into the second half that I realized how incredibly silly I must have seemed.

Standing out there with a uniform that looked like it just came out of the laundry! Taking pleasure in Gatch's compliments when wouldn't the real compliment have been to put me out on the field?

Marshak was lumbering downfield after a pass from Yitzchak. Even after five minutes he was out of shape!

But I probably would have stewed silently if Lupo hadn't picked that moment to come over and give me some advice.

"It's not playink," he said.

"What?"

"Jugglink. Dot's nize. But it doesn't mek you a player."

Who was this clown in his faded madras shirt and baggy flannel pants? This illiterate! This . . . janitor!

"Better than dumping a load of dishes on the floor," I said. "At least I don't trip over my feet like somebody tied my shoelaces together."

Instantly I was sorry. Only Lupo didn't seem to mind.

He laughed, opening his mouth to show me a mouthful of gold teeth. "I saw you dere. Vat were you doink dere?"

"My mother made me go."

"You know Yiddish? I tot you are Cherman."

"My father. My mother, she's from Poland. I mean, my grandparents were."

It was silly, but I could see him look at me like for the first time he felt there was something worth saving. "Hey," he said. "I know you can play dis gem. You can do better than juggling. Dot's all I meant to say."

16

"I think she likes it."

"Oh, she likes it," Alfred said.

"I mean, *she* didn't say stop. *I* stopped. Because I wanted to."

Alfred smiled. This was the next night and I wasn't thinking about soccer. We were sitting on my porch in metal porch chairs. A half-melted carton of banana fudge sat on the glass-topped table between us. Two spoons lay in little pools of chocolate on the glass. "She was at the tennis courts with Kleven all last year," he said. "There and the golf course."

I felt a spasm of jealousy I tried to ignore. "Oh yeah?"

"I don't think they were doing it, though."

"I don't really care."

"All the guys talk about doing it. But most guys aren't. I mean it. Some of these girls, they come to school, they leave one button open on their blouse. You know? So you can see inside? Well, you get them back behind the tennis courts, you gotta have a crowbar to get inside her bra. So anyway, don't feel bad if she doesn't come around. I mean don't expect it. Not right away."

Did he think I didn't know these things? Did he think that just because I was shy I was deaf and blind, too? "What's Barb like?" I said, to show him I could raise topics *he* might be sensitive about.

"She's okay. I mean, no, we fight about it. I'm the one wants to go further."

I had told myself I didn't care. I had told myself I even hoped they were doing it. So I was a little surprised by the sudden surge of triumph rising up in my chest.

"You guys aren't doing it?"

"Howie. Not everything's like *Playboy* magazine."

And that would have annoyed me again except that before I could react, Alfred dropped his superior smile. "Actually," he said, "we don't do much. Not these days."

"Why?"

"Because we're fighting. We fight all the time." For a second I thought he was going to cry.

I knew they had been fighting. Even before the Prom there had been times when I would come up to them standing together in the parking lot during lunch and they would barely say hello, as if I had interrupted something serious. Alfred used to say nice things about Barb; now most of the time I only heard little digs about her weight or her hair or the zit that kept coming back on her chin.

"I never see you fighting."

"Every night. I mean, some days we talk about getting married. Other days we talk about breaking up that night.

I don't want to get married. I always told myself I wasn't going to marry the first person I ever laid. I mean we aren't. Everything but. Hand jobs. Sixty-nine. God. But even so. I'm too young to get married."

Alfred leaned forward, picked up the spoon, and dug into the ice cream. Then I think he did start crying because he just sat there, looking into space, his jaw working, not saying a word until the ice cream started dripping off the spoon onto the table.

17

A few days later I got the same story from Barb. It was Friday, in the middle of June. Ten days away—the Sunday we would play Hercules for the first time—was Alfred's birthday, and I had promised to help Barb put a guest list together ("Howie, I know the girls. But you know the *guys* he likes"). The sun was bright, the leaves on the elms along Prospect Avenue were a light green. It had rained and there was a little breeze rippling puddles in the street. I took a list of seniors from my yearbook file, backed my bike out of the garage, and rode it down Prospect to West Broadway, then along West Broadway to Barb's house, where she was sitting on the front step.

I had known her for years, too. She was dark, with a beautiful face, and except for the one zit on her chin, skin as clear as coffee ice cream, and legs almost as heavy as mine. She was stroking a Siamese cat I had heard her talk about, named If You Please. I coasted onto the sidewalk and braked beside her. *She* was crying.

Startled, she flinched when she saw me.

"Hey. It's only me," I said. "What's wrong?"

She tried to answer. Instead, her face wrinkled up again. She made a mewing sound almost like If You Please, who had jumped away when I came onto the sidewalk and was now slinking around the shrubs on the lawn.

I got off the bike, kicked the kickstand down, and sat on the step beside her.

"You're upset about Alfred," I said.

She swallowed a few times. "Here I am, I'm making this party for him," she said. "And every day I think this is the last day."

"What's the story with you guys, anyway? Who's breaking up with who?"

"Oh. Him with me, I guess. I mean, *I* say we should break up, but it's only because I think he wants to."

She was so open about loving him that it made me jealous. Or rather, it would have made me jealous except that it also made me like her. Sitting there, arms clasped around her knees, Barb looked beautiful and vulnerable—a girl who needed nothing more than someone who would be nice.

"Oh," I said.

"I think all he wants is, I think he, you know, reads—"

"I know you're fighting about sex," I said and flushed.

"I wondered if you did. Alfred told you."

"Last night."

"I don't mind. In fact, I'm glad you do. We're too good friends to keep that secret."

I wanted to hug her. "That's true," I said.

"Anyway, I think that's what bothers him the most. He reads *Playboy* and those awful magazines and he thinks he's got to go out and . . . *screw* the world."

Suddenly I was willing to be disloyal to Alfred. "Let him," I said. "So ten years later he'll wake up and remember you and think what an asshole he was. And some other guy will be lucky and happy because he'll have you."

"You really think that?"

"Sure."

"Sometimes I think I'm not smart enough and also I'm so skinny on top that maybe—"

"You're fine," I said. "You don't have to, um"—I had trouble talking about this casually, but I forced myself to ignore the warmth of my cheeks—"you don't have to go to bed with people if you don't want to."

If You Please had come back. He was rubbing his back against her leg. But she was ignoring him; she was paying strict attention to me. "Thank you," she said.

It was a good thing we were outside where neighbors could see and where cars were driving by, sending water from puddles spraying onto the sidewalk. Because if we had been alone, Alfred or no Alfred—Sandy or no Sandy!—I would have slid over and kissed her.

Did I believe what I said? Knowing that Barb was grateful made me think I believed it. But after I left I rode my bike toward Inwood until I found a little drugstore so seedy, with its faded Breyer's sign and streaked windows, that there wasn't the slightest chance customers would know me. There, trying to look poised, I asked for the three-pack of Trojans in language I had rehearsed over and over since the night before, and as soon as I was home and in my room, slid one of them into my wallet. Just in case. It was in my pocket the next night when I took the Chevy and drove to Sandy's house.

Her father was home. He stood in the driveway making circular sweeps with a chamois over the baby-blue Cadillac Coupe de Ville which only he used, draping some rags over one of the mica boulders at his feet.

By this time I had met him a few times. He was a big man with red skin and an exaggerated version of Sandy's cheekbones—it was as if he had two golf balls implanted below and slightly to the outside of his eyes. He didn't look at all like a man who cared about classical music. He was wearing an old pair of khakis and a sleeveless undershirt. The hair on his chest was a mixture of black and gray. He looked up as I came toward him and surprised me by not smiling at all.

"Hi, Mr. Bessinger," I said.

" 'Lo, Howard."

I looked down at the mica boulders; when I was ten I had decided mica was valuable and had begun collecting the small chunks I could find in the overgrown lot around town. I loved the way they glittered in the sun and the way you could flake the mica and in some cases even peel it where it had formed in large sections.

"These are big," I said. "Where'd you get them?"

"Heavy, too. Bought 'em from a contractor. Sandy's inside," he said, rubbing at a spot on the hood.

"Oh," I said.

He had a smile for Sandy when we came out five minutes later, but here was another surprise: she didn't smile back.

"Which movie you seeing?"

"The Naked Edge."

"*The Naked Edge*. Okay. Okay. Good. A little excitement. Adventure. Don't stay out too late. Or, wait a minute. That's right. You have a new curfew now."

"Daddy."

"Midnight. Or is it later? Let's see."

"See you later, Daddy."

He turned to me, smiling. "What do fathers know?"

But by this time Sandy had already turned and was going down the walk toward the car. I smiled at him and shrugged, then followed her.

"You guys been fighting?" I asked in the car.

Sandy shrugged as if she didn't want to talk about it. But she must have thought that was unfair to me. She settled herself, let me drive for a block while she said nothing to make me understand what was coming up, then said, "My parents are getting divorced."

"Oh."

Remember, this was 1961, when divorces were something for distant relatives and movie stars. I was shocked.

"I don't want to make a big deal about it," Sandy said. "They've talked about this for years, the two of them. Moving out. Now he's going to do it. I think."

"You never mentioned this before."

"They hate each other. But the last six months it got worse. Also, he's closing the store."

"Why?"

"Because of money. He's not making any money on it."

"*Jeez,*" I said, then flushed at how naïve I sounded.

She shrugged. We sat, quietly.

"We can skip the movie," I said. "You want to get a hot dog and just, I don't know. Talk?"

Sandy shook her head. "I need the movie. We've been

fighting all day. Take me to something that makes me forget."

"Okay."

"Not that I don't want to talk about it with you. But not now."

"No problem," I said.

I felt patronized. Wasn't a friend somebody who would sit and listen when things were tough? And maybe interject calming words of advice and find some witty but sympathetic way of restoring order when she got hysterical? How could I be a friend if she wouldn't give me the chance?

But I did what she wanted. After the movie, Sandy herself suggested driving out to the tennis courts. We spent a sweaty hour there during which I took great pride in not going below the waist. I drove her home around midnight without mentioning the divorce once.

That didn't mean I wasn't thinking about it. Alfred's Plymouth was in the street in front of my house; as I pulled into the driveway I was already planning how to tell him. He was sitting on the front porch, the light on, one leg draped over the arm of the porch sofa, eating with a metal spoon out of a half-gallon box of banana fudge.

"Hadda wake your father up," he said. "I needed a spoon."

The street was dark, except for the blue light coming from the upstairs window in Dr. Blumberg's house where the Blumbergs watched television, and as I sat down, that winked out. It was warm for early June. There were no bugs. Prospect Avenue was right off a street filled with stores. But it was also a street with big houses and thick oaks, and there were enough leaves so you could hear the wind rustle them.

"I got something to tell you," I said.

Just then a car turned in off Central and pulled up in

94

the street in front of the house. Sandy got out. "What are you doing here?" I said as she came up the front steps, waving to us through the screen. As I said it another car squealed around the corner. It was the Coupe de Ville. It came to a screeching stop behind Sandy's car.

Mr. Bessinger got out. He took a few steps toward the house but stopped in front of the steps.

"Sandy," he called. "I want you home."

"No."

"*Sandy.*"

She winced. She looked at me. "Are your parents asleep?"

"They were," I said.

Without saying another word, Sandy turned around and went down the steps toward her father. We could hear her whisper something. Then he whispered back. Then she whispered. Then his voice a little louder.

"No," we heard her say.

"That's because you're a slut. A slut. Your mother is, and so are you."

"Daddy! People will hear you!"

Alfred's forehead was furrowed in amazement. Across the street a window flew open. Blumberg's. "I hear you," he called. "Now just you calm down."

"YOU SHUT THE FUCK UP."

"Daddy, why are you doing this?" Sandy wailed. She ran to her car. In a second she was inside, the engine had roared to life, and she peeled away from the curb.

Mr. Bessinger looked around. He looked up at us. He looked across the street at Blumberg's house. Then he walked to his Cadillac and sat behind the wheel. He sat there for almost a minute in the car, then he pulled away, too.

18

"Jesus Christ," Alfred said. "Divorced?"

"That's what she says," I said, looking down to the corner where the cars had disappeared. "Also they're closing the store."

"I knew things were bad," he said. "But not that bad."

"It's awful," I said, nodding soberly.

Actually, I was thrilled. Hadn't she come to me? When she needed somebody, hadn't she raced to her car with no guarantee at all that I was on the porch, and come over to see me?

o   o   o

"Who was that yelling last night?" my father asked the next morning, at breakfast.

"Yelling? What do you mean?"

"I heard yelling. Voke me up. I thought you was out on the porge."

"Must have been early. Before I got home," I said.

We had Sunday off, so Gatch had called a practice. When my father left the table, signaling that breakfast was over, I changed into shorts, took a ball, and went out in the backyard to juggle. It was chilly; the tree from the lot behind our house blocked the sun until noon and the grass was damp.

What if I drove over there? Just pulled up and rang the doorbell and, if Mr. Bessinger answered, ask for Sandy as if nothing at all was new, then take her for a drive and find out what had happened?

96

What stopped me was Sandy. She had seemed so calm when I had picked her up the night before. And there was that little rebuff ("I need the movie") when I pressed her. What if she didn't want anybody comforting her? Wouldn't the most natural thing be to wait for Monday in Yearbook Office in which Sandy and I had taken to spending each afternoon together? Instead I went to practice, where, except for Yitzchak, who smiled and nodded to everybody, no one said a word when I walked onto the field. I took my ball over to one corner of the field and began juggling until it was time for drills.

By this time it was hot. The grass by the sideline was dry. I dribbled a few laps around the field, then started juggling again.

Suddenly I heard the thump of another ball being kicked. I looked up to see a line drive coming at my chest. I caught it with my hands, dropped it to the ground. "You wanna kill me?" I said to Lupo, in shorts and cleats, favoring the ankle, but trotting down the sideline toward me.

He laughed.

"You're all better?"

"Not to play. I try prektice. I vait for the doctor, I vait all goddamn year. Look, you got to stop dis business"—he rolled the ball onto his instep and kept it up on his thighs for a few seconds to show me he could do it—"and play soccer. Come with me."

He took me over to a patch of empty ground in front of the water fountain. Then he dropped the ball at his feet. "Okay," he said. "Take it from me."

It's a game you play all the time: one guy keeps the ball and you try to take it from him. Then you switch. At Lawrence I could hold off two kids at a time, sometimes three

97

when I had the ball, and could get the ball from anybody. Now I watched Lupo roll the ball back with the sole of his right foot, gave him a head fake, and let him circle me. He was limping but not badly. I faked again, but this time I came in one step closer. Lupo moved to his right. Just as he took his foot off the ball I sprang. Weak ankle and all, he was too quick. He nudged the ball to the side, hopped over my foot, and was free.

"Come on," he said. "Try again."

He was dribbling around me again, in a circle. I gave him another fake, moved with him, then tackled again. This time I got my foot on the ball. Lupo moved his shoulder into me and pushed with his foot so the ball went over my foot and then he was by me.

"Dis is vat you god to vork on," he said. "Playink by yourself, dot's like . . ." He moved his fist up and down like a guy jerking off. "Got it?"

"I got it, Lupo."

"You got to know when you *don't* tackle. Just retreat. Cut off the *angle.*"

We worked like that for a half hour. But it wasn't until Gatch whistled us together for a scrimmage that I began to see that Lupo had a plan.

"Play right half today. Not wing," Lupo said.

"Halfback? I'm a wing."

"You vant make first team?"

Suddenly I understood. To play right half would make me the defender who had to cover Marshak. It would give me the chance to play him just the way I had been playing Lupo for the last half hour and a chance to show Gatch how much better I was. A rush of goose bumps went up

98

my arm. I looked at Lupo. He actually looked a little nervous, waiting for my reaction.

"I get it," I said.

He smiled. "You might be just vat ve need."

"But Gatch won't like it," I said.

"It's Gatch's idea," he said.

○ ○ ○

Marshak saw me walk to halfback. He looked at me for a few seconds, then at Lupo. Lupo was looking away. Marshak trotted over to the sideline where Gatch was standing. They talked for a minute, then he came out again and Gatch blew the whistle. Now Marshak knew what was going on.

And give him credit. The first time he got the ball, instead of getting rid of it, he came upfield with it himself and cut in, heading right for me.

Marshak's favorite play was a pass to Sirulnick, who was cutting out to wing. I retreated, moving to Marshak's left. This forced him inside, blocking off any pass to Sirulnick, even though he faked it a few times. Finally he had to get rid of the ball to Bruch, at right wing, who was covered. It was a good pass. Bruch took the ball and moved downfield with it, crossing it into the middle. But when he did I was already back in the penalty area. I leaped, met the ball squarely with my forehead, and sent it downfield about forty yards.

"Good head," Gatch called, from the sidelines.

○ ○ ○

Again, only eighteen men had shown up. With nine on a side you had to run more. But Marshak was reading plays so well he could loaf and save his energy. He got by me once dribbling. I took the ball from him once. After that he would give me a fake, then cut inside, dribbling slowly, looking for a free man or passing back.

Meanwhile, I was playing him man for man, harassing him when he had the ball. I would make mistakes, counting on being quick enough to recover, but it made him look smooth and in control.

Then, about twenty minutes into the scrimmage, Yitzchak broke up a play way down by their goal, passed up to Marshak, and I was on him before he could get rid of the ball; he made a bad pass. He had to race back to the end line again. The ball came to him and instead of trapping it, which would have meant running with the ball, having to screen it from my tackling, Marshak tried to first-time it. He got part of his shoe on the ball, the ball went about twenty yards, curved, went out of bounds, and I knew he was tired.

I looked over at the sidelines. Gatch was talking to somebody, but his eyes were on the field.

The throw-in came to me. I tried to chip the ball over Marshak's head to my wing, who was cutting in behind him. The pass was good, but my wing let it hit off his shin and it came to Marshak again. I was about ten yards away. I moved in. Marshak saw me and began moving left with the ball. I moved with him, letting him come closer, but then taking a few steps back as if I were retreating to slow him down. Marshak lengthened his stride again, and as the ball came off his foot I went in, got my foot on the ball, and moved it over the top of his shoe just like Lupo had done to me an hour before.

After that it was easy. Any ball in Marshak's area had me going for it, full speed, knowing Marshak would take three steps, then back off. When I had the ball I could dribble, knowing he was too tired to do anything but fake a tackle. Once I stopped, put the ball under my foot, and said, "Come on, Marshak. Come on. Take it."

"Asshole," he gasped.

"Come on." Even at that moment a corner of my mind could be surprised and guilty at the hatred and exultation in my voice. "Come on. Take it from me."

He lunged. I went by him.

Gatch blew his whistle. "Okay. Enough for today."

Marshak was bent over, hands on his knees, panting and looking at the ground. I dribbled toward the sideline and passed the ball to Gatch, who had the mesh practice ball bag in his hand. He looked at me. Shaw and Bruch came up and said something. He said something back. Then he motioned to me. I walked over to him, then followed him out onto the field, walking toward Marshak.

"I should say this to both of you," he said.

Marshak stood up. And that was when I stopped hating him. He looked at Gatch, his chest heaving, and with nobody within yards, said, "You mean me?" sounding like a kid in second grade.

"Louis," Gatch said—it was the first time I had heard anybody call him by his first name—and put a hand on his shoulder. "We've given you a lot of chances."

Marshak looked at me, then at Gatch.

"Lose twenty pounds more, maybe you can beat the kid out. But not now. Not for weeks. I'm gonna start him on Saturday."

I expected Marshak to say something—swear, punch Gatch in the chest—but he nodded. Sweat pouring down his face caught in the gray stubble on his chin. "Ya. Ya, you right," he said. He turned away. But then he turned back to me, and you could see how much this cost him by the way his lips tightened and he started a few times before he could get anything out.

"Congratulations," he said.

The rest of the team watched, arms folded, as the three of us walked toward the sidelines. Nobody said a word to me. Well, who needed them? At least, who needed anything more than the wink Lupo flashed as I passed him on the way to the parking lot. Who needed to feel guilt?

But ahead of me Marshak walked alone, toward his car, socks rolled down around his ankles, dirt on his calves from a spill he had taken inside the penalty area where the grass was already worn away.

If you asked me what traffic was like as I drove the Chevy back to Cedarhurst, I couldn't have told you; I was too busy rehearsing the way I would tell the story to Alfred and Dad and anyone else who would listen ("And Gatch, he says, 'We've given you a lot of chances' "). It wasn't until I passed Mill Road that I remembered Sandy, and now I felt more confident.

Need me? Of course she needed me! Who wouldn't need somebody who had just taken on a former All-Warsaw left wing and run him into the ground? I turned down Addison Street to Sandy's house and parked in front, opening the door and swinging my feet into the street to unlace my cleats in case she asked me to come inside. Someone pulled the living room curtain back. Sandy's face appeared in the window. A moment later she came outside, ran down the steps, and got in the car.

"Drive around the block," she said.

"Okay."

That annoyed me. Here I'd driven over to comfort her and she barked orders at me like a female Jimmy Cagney.

"First of all," she said as I pulled into the street, "I'm sorry about last night. My father was a complete ass."

"Oh, I don't know—"

"He was. But so was I. I just wanted to— I just needed a friend. But letting him follow me and start yelling. God. I was so embarrassed. I thought I'd die. I *am* embarrassed. He doesn't know what he's saying."

She wasn't crying. But she was trembling. Should I pull over? Should I put my arms around her, or would that just make her mad? I kept driving, darting glances at her out of the corner of my eye. Sandy wasn't wearing lipstick, and a black sleeveless blouse and black pair of bermudas made her look pale. Her fingernails were bitten. As I glanced over, she raised her hand as if to nip off a hangnail. Then she yanked her hand away, put it in her lap, and began picking at it with her other hand. I realized that to her this kind of confession took nerve.

"Look," I said, "I'm *glad* you came over."

"Do you want me to apologize to your parents?"

"You don't have to apologize to my parents. They didn't even hear him."

"They must've—"

"And if they did, it wasn't your fault." And now I did pull the car over, ramming the shift up into PARK and turning to face her. "If you get upset about something I want you to call me up or come over. That's what friends are for."

The way her forehead smoothed out and she stopped picking her finger was every bit as dramatic as I could hope.

"You really are a friend," she said.

103

19

She was in the stands on Sunday, but the only way I knew was to look where I had told her to sit; for the first time that year the stands were full.

There were twice as many Greeks as Jews. Most of the Greeks were men, their straight black hair brushed straight back and parted in the middle or not at all. There were so many of them they spilled over onto the grass beside the bleachers and even onto the far sideline. But there were families, too. The women came carrying baskets and blankets, wearing long peasant dresses of red or violet. Knots of kids swarmed around them. The Jews, on the other hand, were almost all men, almost all older than me, about half wearing yarmulkas.

Sandy was about five rows up, sitting on the Jewish side. The night before, we had gone out for a malted with Alfred and Barb—a kind of pre-birthday celebration marking us as better friends than the gang coming to the party—and afterward Sandy and I had spent two hours on my porch talking. I waved to her, then turned back to the field.

The Greeks looked tough. For this game the park groundskeepers had taken the trouble to set up extra benches for the teams. Christofilakos, who had stopped playing a week early so the first team could get more time with his replacement, was standing by the Hercules bench in street clothes, dark and good-looking, his pink shirt worn outside black chinos. He smiled and waved every few seconds, and when

104

somebody yelled to him in Greek, obviously telling him he belonged on the field, he would shrug his shoulders and look grateful.

The rest of the team looked younger than Maccabiah by about ten years. They stood in little clusters, juggling or heading to each other, wearing blue uniforms with white letters and numbers—since Israel and Greece have the same national colors, our uniforms were reversed. None of the Greeks wore shin guards.

I was hoping there would be a little murmur when I walked out with the starting team, but there wasn't. Marshak sat down by the bench. Lupo and Gatch, both in street clothes, stood together. It was hot again; I could feel the heat where the plastic of the number on the back of my uniform clung to my skin.

"Hey, Jewboy. We gonna give it to you today," one of their forwards said as we shook hands. He was grinning.

By this time I was used to it. "We'll give it to you," I said. "We'll give it to you Greek." That meant something sexual; I didn't know exactly what, but I'd heard people say it. It was supposed to get the Greek guys mad. But this one only laughed. Then the whistle blew.

○ ○ ○

The Greeks were playing a 4–2–4. Four fullbacks, two halfbacks, and four forwards. We were in the 4–3–3 more popular in 1961: four fullbacks but three halfbacks and three forwards. With one less forward we would shoot less, but the extra halfback meant our midfield had to run less. A good thing. Without Lupo and except for Yitzchak, they were ten years past their prime. For the first ten or fifteen minutes, both sides played cautiously. When a Greek halfback got the ball he would stand on it, then move slowly upfield, keeping the ball on the ground, not hesitating to pass back if he got into trouble. Then all of a sudden one of the wings would cut in and there would be a long pass, floating over Yitzchak's head into the penalty area. Goldstein would have to cut inside behind Yitzchak to head the ball out.

They were testing us. And if the crowd didn't know I was new, Hercules did. When the ball came to me for the first time, they would test me, too.

It came on a pass out to me from Goldstein, on the ground. I moved to the ball, but I could hear one of the Greeks behind me as I cushioned it on my shoe. I gave him a head fake, as if I was going with the ball, then trapped it and cut inside.

The Greek cut with me. He was playing me tight. To get away I had to cut into the middle of the field where I didn't want to go. "*Paz* id! *Paz* id! *Paz* id!" I heard somebody calling. Stein. But to get the ball over to him I would have had to chip it over this guy's head, and I wasn't sure I could do that. His cleats thumped into the ground. His breath rasped. I dribbled almost to the end of the penalty box and then, not knowing who was open, wheeled, chipped a pass out to the wing, figuring Bruch was there. He was, but the pass was rushed. It went over the end line.

"Take your time," Lupo called to me from the sidelines as I ran back up toward the midfield line.

I made a circle with my thumb and forefinger. I was breathing hard, but I glanced around to look at the back who was on me. He was a short dark man with a beard, a little chubby and very quick. As I watched, Goldstein intercepted a pass. But it bounced off his shin about five yards away. The Greek moved right in, picked the ball up, gave him a good fake, and was by him.

106

And minutes later, they scored.

Goldstein's fault. He went out to tackle one of their insides when he had the space to retreat. He missed the tackle, which gave them a two on one against Stein, and while Goldstein was racing to get back into position the inside chipped a little pass over Goldstein's head and the Greek first-timed it past Rabinowitz.

There was a roar from the bleachers. The Greek forward who had scored jumped into the air again and again, both fists in the air, arms bent at the elbows. The rest of the team converged on him, while from the sidelines, young men in black pants and black shirts and purple rayon jackets ran out on the field to hug him.

"Ged it back," Lupo called as we walked back into position.

But we didn't right away. When the whistle blew, Bruch passed back to Yitzchak, who sent a low curving pass to me.

Anyway, it was supposed to come to me. As I lifted my foot a blue shirt hurtled past me, took it on the inside of his thigh, and after two steps had the ball on the ground, under control. Looking around, he dribbled a few steps, changing direction about three times, then passing out to *his* wing. It was the one with the beard.

This time I took careful look. He wasn't somebody I recognized from the year before. He was young, maybe a few years older than me, dark and round-faced under his beard, with dark hairy legs and dusty Puma cleats on a pair of very small feet.

"Move to the ball, Howie." This time it was Gatch from the sidelines.

Was I really that slow? Suddenly I was scared in a way I had never been during a game.

And for the next forty minutes I didn't do a thing right.

He wouldn't let me. When the ball came to me he was tackling even if I looked in control. If I gave him a fake he would recover fast or ignore it. He had a way of shepherding me to the outside, then anticipating me when I heeled the ball back, and one time he cut in back of me, took the ball away, boomed it downfield where one of their forwards took it on his chest, wheeled, and shot just wide of the goal.

"Get *rid* of it!" Gatch would call to me. "Get rid of the ball!"

"Goddamnit, Berger. Don't you know dis game?" someone else yelled at me.

Knowing that Sandy was looking at me, I smiled as if this was the way teammates always talked to each other. My legs ached and I was out of breath even though I wasn't working hard. *Settle down, settle down,* I tried to tell myself. But there was a jumpy, grapefruit-sized lump of fear spreading through my stomach and into my groin. I began to pray that the ball wouldn't come to me.

Yet I could see not everything was my fault. For some reason the balls that came to me were coming from our fullbacks instead of from Yitzchak. They were coming in the air, great booming kicks, which meant that our midfield was out of position except for Yitzchak, who was up and back, carrying on defense and distributing the ball cleverly on offense.

But I was too scared to think about that. On defense I started to lay off. If the ball fell between me and a Greek I would do a quick three steps toward the ball, then back off just like Marshak. Hercules saw that, and now they began coming up the right side all the time.

"Go to him, Howie. *Go* to him."

But I didn't. Not that time. And the next time, telling myself I had to make a tackle, I moved at just the wrong time and he was by me.

"Who is that guy?" I asked when the half-time whistle blew and we walked toward the bench.

Nobody answered. Stein was stretched out on the ground. The rest of the team were walking slowly across the sideline and dropping down on the grass alongside him or sitting on the bench. Gatch was walking around, passing out orange slices from a brown A&P shopping bag.

"Ve all got somebody," Bruch said, finally.

Was he that good? Or was it just that I wasn't as good as I thought, a hot shit in high school who looked ordinary as soon as he came up against some good athletes who had spent their lives playing soccer? I expected Gatch to come up, put his hand on my shoulder, and tell me Marshak was starting again.

But he didn't. About ten minutes into the second half we tied it up. It was a fluke. One of our guys tried a shot from outside the penalty area just as one of their fullbacks was looking in another direction. The ball hit his hand and dropped at his feet. The ref called a penalty shot and Stein scored, accompanied by a deafening thunder of boos.

Now it was the Jews' chance to cheer.

"Defense! Defense!" Gatch shouted from the sidelines.

I moved back to give us a little more defense. After all, wasn't it an upset even to tie Hercules? In three years we hadn't even come close to a tie.

For the next twenty minutes we played the kind of game we had never played before. Again and again Hercules would bring the ball up, passing cautiously, keeping the ball on the ground, then finally crossing into the middle, where Bruch or Goldstein would head the ball out to a halfback. I would race madly upfield. Our halfback would boom it in the air about twenty yards beyond, not caring about anything except that the ball was away from our goal. Then Hercules would bring it up again.

They got their shots. The balls went wide. They bounced off the crossbar. They came low into the goal and Rabinowitz saved them with diving lunges. They came high and he leaped, arms outstretched, to tip the ball back over the goal.

Most of the Hercules shots came from the new man. He was a halfback. But when he saw the way our halfbacks were clearing the ball he began playing up, cutting ahead of his own forwards to take passes from the other halfbacks. So I began playing even farther back and cutting more toward the center.

And that was why I was almost in our penalty area when he took a pass, cut into the middle, and came right at me.

"Back! Get back!" someone shouted at me.

I came up at the guy. He slowed and gave me a head fake. I didn't go for it. Then he put his foot on the ball and, as I stopped, he moved again, very quickly, and passed me on the left.

I recovered. By this time I was rattled. I stuck a foot out. But he was by me. I raced after him. But now he and a forward had a two-on-one on Goldstein. A pass. Return pass. Then he had a clear shot, me right behind him, almost stepping on his heel, dimly aware of Rabinowitz, hunched over in the middle of the goal, brows furrowed, concentrating on the ball but with yards of space on either side of him, and that was when I got so angry I stuck my arm out and shoved the Greek so he tripped and went sprawling.

"FOUL! FOUL!" the Greeks began shouting in English.

110

A great, swelling thunder of boos came from the stands. The whistle blew. I looked around to see the ref pointing at me. Right behind him was Lupo, standing on the end line, face in his palms, wailing, "Oy. Berger, *asshole*! Ass*hole*!"

Rabinowitz, sweat trickling down through the black and gray stubble as he leaned forward, dove left for the penalty shot. The ball went like an air-to-air missile into the right side of the net. Hercules went on defense. We played out the game, not even getting close to scoring. When we walked off the field not even Gatch bothered to go over to me.

20

"Forget about me?"

There were still some people on the field, but not many. I was sitting by myself on the grass, and when I heard Sandy's voice, I cringed.

I hadn't forgotten about her. In fact I even knew that, having driven here with her, I would have to take her back and maybe go shopping for some joke presents for Alfred's party that night. To talk with her was something else. I had been sitting there alone for almost fifteen minutes; the point was that if I could look lonely but stoic, bearing my shame with a kind of manly grace, maybe, just maybe, she would chalk the foul up to some inexplicable masculine ethic and be willing to respect me again.

"Oh. Hi," I said.

She had a pink sweater tied around her waist. She was

wearing bermudas again, but these were white and against them her legs looked brown. "Boy, the last few minutes," she said. "I didn't know what was going on. Somebody had to explain it."

"Explain what? How I completely screwed things up?"

She made no pretense about denying it. "How did it happen? You just lose your temper?"

"I was so *frus*trated. But I've never done that in my life. Pushing a guy in the penalty zone."

"Well, next time you won't do it. That's how you learn."

For a second I couldn't believe she was taking it so calmly. Didn't she know I had completely destroyed things? The chance to take over first place? My chance to start? For all I knew, Gatch would never put me in a game again.

"If there is a next time."

"He didn't fire you," Sandy said.

Which was ridiculous, of course, and I almost said so. Why fire me when he could put me back on the second team? I looked to see if she thought it was a joke, but she wasn't smiling.

And suddenly I realized something. Why should she? How could she know how awful I was? Any more than I would know what mistakes she made when she played Chopin in school assembly?

"Want to get Carvel?"

There was something so comforting in her voice that suddenly I didn't care whether I played again.

So I'd go to Cornell! So I'd become a doctor and go to labs and put my soccer ball away every winter. Wouldn't it be worth it if there was Sandy to visit in New York? Couldn't I see myself getting on a bus out of Ithaca, throwing my bag onto the overhead rack, and taking the ride into New

112

York each weekend to see a girl who loved me?

"I'm starved," I said.

"Dad left last night," she said so casually I knew it must have been rehearsed.

21

If there was anything wrong between Alfred and Barb you couldn't tell it from the house. A giant HAPPY BIRTHDAY, ALFRED cut out of yellow crepe paper hung stretched between the two elm trees on Barb's front lawn. Barb's mother was inside when we came in the door. She smiled and pointed us downstairs to the basement.

I followed Sandy downstairs. Against the far wall Barb had set up a long table, on top of which were glass and plastic bowls of pretzels and potato chips and little blue cereal bowls of dip. There was a large bowl of red punch; Alicia Braunstein, one of Barb's best friends, was ladling herself some punch into a little cone-shaped paper cup.

"Well, look who's here," Barb called.

"Hi," I said.

"Hi, Barb," Sandy said.

Barb was standing by a record player flipping through a stack of 45s. She picked up about half of them, slipped them onto the converter, pushed a button, and all of a sudden the basement was filled with the Drifters singing "There Goes My Baby."

o   o   o

Mr. Bessinger had left the night before. It was for good, Sandy had told me after the game as we drove out of the parking lot. He had packed two suitcases and taken the Cadillac to a motel in Syosset. Before he did, though, there had been an argument which lasted most of the night and which had made it impossible to hate him. Along with threats about money and accusations had come tears and guilt ("God *knows* I've made mistakes!") and a moment in which he had fallen on his knees to apologize to Sandy for his outburst in front of my house. The week before, Sandy was pretending things were under control. Now it was different.

"We just don't know what's happening," Sandy said.

"Whatever it is," I said maturely, "you'll be all right."

"I'll live. Sure. But money? We don't know about money. Mom says she doesn't know what he'll pay for food or tuition. Besides, Howie, I love my father. Seeing him on his knees. Crying. *She's* crying. One time he pulls out their wedding picture and makes her look at it. Then all three of us start crying."

"That's terrible," I said. In fact that did frighten me. Could I imagine my father leaving? Pulling down the wedding picture that hung in that black metal frame above their bed, packing a suitcase, and taking the Buick into the city to check into a hotel?

We had gone to Carvel, to my house, where I took a quick shower and changed, then drove over to her house.

Nobody was home but I didn't kiss her. Somehow it didn't seem right, the way copping a feel at a funeral wouldn't have been right.

"My mom's at her sister's," Sandy said.

By this time I had mentioned the divorce to my parents and knew that grown-ups had a hard time too. "How's she doing?" I asked.

"She was crying all last night. The things she *told* me."

And if there was the impulse to follow that up ("Oh yeah? Like what things?"), I only nodded in the compassionate way I thought adult and said, "Mm."

I had a vision of the two of us slumping down on the living room couch and talking for hours, but when we came through the living room Sandy switched on the lamp behind the piano, then sat down. At first she hit a few notes and chords as if she just wanted to play a few notes. Then, almost as if I wasn't there, she launched into a piece.

For a second it made me angry. I sat down on the couch, putting one leg over the arm. Sandy flipped through the pages of a yellow book that said *Mozart* on the cover.

Only then she must have realized what she was doing because she closed the book. "Oh. Hey," she said. "Remember what you said? About playing pop?"

"Mm," I said, but not compassionately.

"I got a surprise for you." She started banging away loudly with her right hand. For a second I didn't know what she was playing. But then I jumped up. With one arm out, the other brushing my pants leg as if I held a guitar, I started stamping my foot and singing in my best Chuck Berry voice.

At that point she started laughing so hard she couldn't play. "What do you think?"

" 'Roll Over Beethoven,' " I said. "It's terrific. How'd you like my singing?"

"Good. You really like it?"

"Sure. It sounds just like the record."

"I got the music last week," she said. Standing, she opened the piano bench and took out a sheaf of piano music. "This stuff is easy. It's such garbage it takes about a half hour. I can do it from the chords. Listen to this one."

115

"Goodness, gracious, great balls of fire," I sang. I held my crotch, but she was looking down at the keys. She didn't play this one through either, but jumped up from the piano. "That's going to be my project this summer. I don't want to dance to this garbage. But at least I'll be able to, you know, play it for the kids."

After hearing her echo my words so precisely, how could I feel left out? "You can play it right now," I said.

o o o

Now, at the party, I saw her listening to the Drifters as if for the first time.

"That's pretty," she said.

"You could play it."

"I could play it. The big surprise is, I'm starting to like it. You think maybe there's some money in this?"

"Prob'ly. Prob'ly a lot of money."

"Maybe later we can go back to my house and look through music. Mom won't be home till about two. They're talking. My aunt's been divorced twice."

About ten couples were at the party already. There were Joan Friedberg and Marty Oestreich. Joan had gone to grade school with us and now went to Woodmere Academy. There were Steve Schumacher and Janie Herbst and Mike Ciparelli and some girl I didn't know. Mike was the only Italian we invited to parties, and he invariably brought along an Italian girl from Inwood who would stick to him and smile uncomfortably all evening.

Some of the kids began to dance. Sandy and I made our way across the basement to Alfred.

"Want some punch?"

"I'll give you a punch," Alfred said.

116

○ ○ ○

In about an hour there were thirty kids in the basement. At one point we all had to give Alfred little joke presents, which had been my responsibility to grinningly set up during the week. Then Barb put out all the lights and came downstairs with a cake, the candles lit, giving her face a golden color. We sang "Happy Birthday" ("Hey, Sandy. Where's your piano?"), then the lights came on again and we crowded around the long table while Alfred flourished a cake knife and cut thin slices of cake with the surprising precision of a neurosurgeon, ladling them onto paper plates with the knife.

When Alfred finished the last slice there was a round of applause and Barb kissed him.

How could she? How could she possibly when I had seen her crying her eyes out a week before? How could they smile and hold hands and each night fight like commandos? I looked around. Sandy was on the other side of the room, her face serious, talking with or anyway listening to Mike Ciparelli. Suddenly I wanted to leave. I wanted us to be alone, in the front seat of the Chevy, holding each other and talking the way we had been during the week.

I walked over to Sandy, taking pride in the easy way I could nod to Mike and butt right into the conversation.

"Let's go," I said.

She giggled. "Can we? Excuse us, Mike."

"By all means," he said. He walked off.

"But can we?" Sandy asked. "Really. Alfred's your best friend. It's his party."

"That's how come we can go," I said. "Be*cause* he's my best friend."

"Okay. Let's."

117

And probably we would have gone except at that moment there was the clumping sound of somebody coming down the stairs.

"Oh, God," Sandy said.

Gene Kleven was tall, skinny, and good-looking in his crew cut, chinos, penny loafers with white socks, and a white letter sweater that would have been too warm for June except that it had an *S* on it, the purple and gold *S* of Syracuse.

He came downstairs, looked around, and waved to Barb and Alfred, gave Mike Ciparelli a little punch on the shoulder. Then he saw Sandy and his eyebrows lifted and he strode across the room, parting the couples in front of him (" 'Scuse me. Thanks. Hey, how are ya. Heah, home for a week"). "Hey, Sandy. Wondered if you'd be here," he said.

"Hi," she said. "Gene, like you to meet Howie Berger. Howie, this is Gene Kleven."

"Oh, Howie. We know each other," he said. "How's the soccer?"

"Okay."

"Only sport where you dribble a ball with your feet. Amazing. So how are you?"

"Fine," Sandy said.

Because I was so upset I had to pretend I wasn't. I looked around, like a celebrity at a party. "Listen," I said. "I gotta see somebody." Before either of them could object I was over by the record player where Mike Ciparelli was standing with his date. "Hey. How ya doin'," I said.

They talked for maybe ten minutes. Kleven did most of the talking while she nodded. But there were times when he was listening, running a hand nervously through his flattop or jamming both fists into the pockets of the letter sweater

118

while she talked. Once he said something and she interrupted him angrily. But then he said something and grinned and she laughed.

After a while I forced myself not to look. I picked up the stack of records and began flipping through them. There were about fifty in the pile, Dot, Decca, Sun, Roulette, some fitted with yellow plastic adapters. To flip through them was to flip through the biggest hits of the last three years.

At last I set them on the table and walked back across the room.

". . . Then I'm going back up," Kleven was saying. "Talk to you." Seeing me, he grinned and punched me lightly on the shoulder. As if he had really come to wish Alfred a happy birthday, he moved off to where Alfred was standing with Barb.

Sandy turned to me. "Let's get out of here," she said.

She was upset. I could see it in the way she raced through her good-byes to a surprised Alfred and Barb, looking only at them; and then in the way her smile disappeared once we were upstairs past the door and a nervous, hovering Mrs. Olman. The night air felt cool and fresh, and after two hours of Little Richard and Bill Haley everything was suddenly very quiet.

"Where do you want to go?" I asked once we were in the car.

"Anywhere."

Should I just take her home? Take her to the door and leave her? But that would just make it clear that I was jealous. "The tennis courts?"

"Sure."

I didn't say anything, as if stopping for stop signs and

119

slowing for the turnoff at Causeway, then fishing for the quarter to get us over the Atlantic Beach Bridge took all my concentration.

By the toll gate the silence had lasted so long it was clear we had to talk about it. "Did that bother you? Seeing him?" I asked finally as the tires hit the metal part of the bridge.

"He's a bastard," she said. "He came there trying to upset me."

"Sandy. How?"

"Oh. It takes too long to explain. Really. But one thing I'll tell you. I'm not seeing him anymore."

This time my silence lasted long enough for the car to cross over to concrete. The sound of the tires changed from a whine to a purr.

"Really?"

"I just don't want to see him anymore."

"Did he ask you, um, did he ask you out?"

"He didn't ask me out. He made a point of telling me about some girl he was going out with. Girl up at Syracuse. I happen to know he's seen her twice."

How did she know? And what was that satisfied note in her voice?

Sandy slid across the seat and kissed my shoulder. She put a hand on my neck. "I'm sorry," she said.

"It's okay."

"No. I mean it. I shouldn't be talking about him. You looked good tonight."

She was doing it to placate me. Even so, she said it so casually it was hard not to believe she meant it. "Me?"

"No. The guy in the backseat. Yeah, you. I hate crew cuts."

120

"It's like having a toothbrush on your head."

She began scratching the back of my head. "There's nothing to run your hand through."

After we found a space at the courts I turned to Sandy and put my arms around her, moving them around to her back and along her arms and feeling her rib cage underneath the blouse. She hugged me tightly, rubbing her head against my neck and then kissing me so long I had to breathe through my nose.

Then she started to moan, a low sighing noise from back in her throat that scared me for a second until I realized it was what had been described so many times in *Dude*. This time when I unbuttoned her blouse she didn't stop me. I was afraid I would fumble with her bra strap in back, but it was easy. The bra came off and I pushed it up and I was looking at real breasts for the first time in my life, even though it was hard to see them in the gloom. I could stroke the nipples and feel them get bigger.

"Bg sit," I said.

"Wha'?"

"Let's get in the backseat."

"Okay."

But when we had scrambled over the top and were kissing and I had moved my hands under her skirt, Sandy stopped me and sat up. "Wait," she said.

"Why?"

She glanced at her watch. Then she held her wrist up. The moonlight glinted off the crystal but it wasn't enough. "Can't see," she said. "Listen. Do you, um, have protection?"

This was a Five Towns girl? This was a Jewish girl when I had been told that with Jewish girls it might take a year to even get them to take off their clothes? Or was it just that Gene had hurt her tonight and this was her way of getting him back?

"Sandy, you want to do it?"

"You want to, don't you? Let's go back to my house."

"Only if you really want to," I said.

Now there was a long silence. Sandy looked up at me, then down into the darkness at the floorboards. It was warm inside the car.

"You think it's because of Gene," she said.

"Gene or something he said. This means you, uh, slept with him, not that I mind, it's your right to do it, but probably what he said tonight had something to do with it."

"Well, it did," she said. "All that talk about his girl friend in Syracuse. So *stupid.* It made me realize we had an empty house tonight and somebody who is good to me the way he never was and I was wasting it. So it *was* something he said."

It wasn't the most perfect answer. For one thing it was too simple. And what was so appealing about my being "good" to her? Did people like Steve McQueen because he was good?

But by now I felt foolish. Here was my chance to do it and, in one unexpected stroke of luck, vault over Alfred and every other virgin. And what was I doing? Stalling!

"You guys broke up? Really?"

"I should've done it months ago."

She dropped a hand onto my thigh as she said that. And just then a car came down the path, its lights still on. For a second Sandy's face and breasts lit up, and even the chance to look at two perfect breasts and two pinkish brown nipples peeking out from underneath her loosened bra was not as

122

important as seeing the furrowed face of a girl who had to be reassured she had said the right thing.

"I got a safe," I said, trembling. "You really want to go to your house?"

22

It was dark and she led me upstairs by the hand. Her bedroom was on the second floor, a small room with an assortment of pine bookcases, a little desk, and a four-poster single bed in the center with a little pink canopy. On the walls, pictures of Sandy playing piano alternated with framed posters of recitals. She pulled the drapes, turned around smiling, I put my arms around her and forgot all about Gene Kleven.

Taking your clothes off in front of a girl? The question had bothered me constantly when I was eleven and first learned that men did such things. I remembered it now as I took off my chinos and shirt and stood in front of Sandy in my underpants, wondering whether to fold things up or leave them tangled on the floor.

Sandy was standing in her bra and bermudas. "On the floor is fine," she said, whispering even though no one was home.

"Okay," I whispered back and dropped them.

Sandy took a step back, reaching to turn off the overhead light. Then she took the rest of her clothes off and we got into bed together.

And after that, what do I remember? I remember how wet she felt when I put my hand between her legs, and how

123

exciting that was. I remember having to get up again for my wallet and how the Trojan unrolled just the way I had practiced. And I remember being inside, hearing her mutter "Ohh" with such a sharp intake of breath I didn't know whether I had hurt her, and thinking to myself again, *Am I really doing this?*

I remember lying with Sandy afterward, her head on my chest, the Trojan curled up on the night table, me as happy as if I'd won every juggling contest in the world.

I'd done it! And gracefully! When I had withdrawn, Sandy—who for all I knew had done it *hundreds* of times, a thought which even then inspired a flicker of anger—had smiled and reached down to stroke my penis in a gesture that looked almost grateful.

My eyes grew heavy, though the knowledge that in an hour her mother would be home kept me awake. After a while I lifted my head and looked over across the bed.

"You awake?"

Sandy's eyes were wide open. She was staring past the canopy toward the window. Her pupils were bright with reflected light. Tears were running down her cheeks into her neck.

23

"What's wrong?"

With a convulsive movement, Sandy jerked her head to the side so I couldn't see her face. I put my hand on her arm. She shrugged it off and sat up on the edge of the bed.

"Sandy. What is it?"

"Daddy's right," she said. "I'm a slut."

Even then I could see a touch of melodrama. There was melodrama in the slight way she hesitated after saying, "Daddy's right," to keep me in suspense. But the tears were real. And now they were accompanied by great, gasping sobs that started high and finished low, then started high again as she took a shuddering breath.

"What do you *mean*? Sandy! What are you *say*ing?"

"He said I was a s-s-slut. He's right."

"Why?"

"Eighteen years old and I've slept with two guys. What do *you* call it?"

"I call it fine."

"Fine? You call it fine? We've gone on three dates and we're sleeping together? You call that fine?"

She began again, this time so loudly I would have asked her if the neighbors could hear except it would have seemed like I was concerned about myself.

"This isn't the nineteenth century, Sandy," I said. "This is America. Nineteen sixty-one in the United States of *America*. You can do what you want to."

"You *can't* do what you want to."

"Why not?"

"Because people look at you. People judge you. That's why not."

"Well, I'm judging us. I think we're innocent."

"Don't joke, Howie. Don't be a sophist." She started crying again.

"I'm just telling you why something that was your idea—"

"It's not my idea."

"I beg to differ. *You* wanted to go to bed with me."

"HOWIE, I WAS UPSET. I DID IT BECAUSE I WAS UPSET."

"About what?"

"About Gene. I saw Gene and I got upset. Okay?"

In an instant the pride I felt at being naked in bed with a girl shriveled.

"You did this to get back at Gene?"

"What do you care? Now you did it. Now you can go to Alfred and tell him. That's what you wanted. Isn't it?"

"It most certainly was not," I said.

Oh, I hated her. She was right. Her father was right. She was a slut. She had been saying those things and doing those things to me and all she was thinking about was Gene Kleven.

"It's that girl, right?" I said. "His girl up in Syracuse. Right?"

She was silent.

"Answer me."

What was the best thing? Should I just get out of bed, look around for my pants, put them on, and go downstairs without saying a word? Should I wait a few seconds and then give her a long speech, talking about all the ways she hadn't measured up and all the long-range problems I saw in store for her? ("Well, I hope you're happy. I really do, San. But I don't think you will be. You see . . .")

But instead I lay there, hoping that she would somehow take it all back. And she did.

"No," she said.

"No, what?"

"No, it didn't bother me. Not much anyhow. I didn't mean what I said."

"Said about what?"

126

"About being upset. I am *upset*. But you're right. I f— I slept with you because I wanted to."

"So why did you say that? Jeez, Sandy. That really hurts. You know that?"

She started to cry again. Now I sat up, pushing my back up against the headboard and putting a hand on her shoulder. "Hey, Sandy. Don't cry. Don't cry, Sandy."

She reached underneath the night table and pulled up a Kleenex from somewhere and blew her nose. "I read all those books, too," she said. "The beatniks, all talking about free love. But boys *do* want to marry a virgin. Gene did. We talked about it. *You* do."

"Marry a virgin? Not me."

"Really?"

"Oh, Sandy. Taking a girl's virginity hurts. I don't want to hurt her."

"It doesn't always hurt," Sandy said, automatically, making me jealous. In fact, I knew that I wanted to marry a virgin; I agreed with Alfred. The trick was to get one that had broken her hymen, say, from riding a horse.

"That's true," I said. "But for some it does."

She wasn't finished crying. She turned around, crossing her legs on the bed so she was sitting Indian-style, but looking down while she got her voice under control. "Guys say that. But they don't mean it, Howie. You should hear what my girl friends say. The *fights* they've had with boys. I *mean* it."

"Well, that's others. Not me."

Sandy's breasts weren't large, but when she leaned over, they hung and swayed a little, the nipples erect. There were little moles and beauty marks on her chest and some on

127

her arms. She seemed totally unconscious that she was sitting there, exposing a patch of pubic hair, and that I couldn't keep my eyes off of it.

I wanted her to love me! What's more, she did! Oh, sure, she had said something that hurt me, but did that mean it was true? If it was true, why did she rattle on and on with me in the Yearbook Office? Why laugh at my jokes? Why say nice things ("I think you're terrific")?

"We have to get up," Sandy said. She pointed to a white electric alarm clock on the night table.

"I'm sorry you had such a rotten time," I said.

She shook her head. "I had a *good* time, Howie. No doubt about it. I loved this. But it scares me that I did. I don't want to be a nympho."

"You're no nympho."

She reached over and took my hand. "I'm sorry I'm such a drip."

"Because you were crying?"

She smiled to show me she got the joke. "Because when people, um, go to bed with each other it's not supposed to be like this."

Don't be naïve, I warned myself. Don't believe something because you want to believe it.

"Like what?"

"Making you feel bad. All this crying. Which is dumb, because I . . . I *had* a good time."

"Did you really? The truth."

"Yes. I know what I said, Howie. About Gene and all. But I wanted this. Really."

"Really?"

"Really." She smiled and reached over, touched my chest. "You're getting hair."

128

I was embarrassed. Guys were supposed to be happy if they had a hairy chest. Actually, I had liked mine when it was smooth. Kleven's was smooth. "Starting to," I said.

"Does that happen late? With guys, I mean."

"Later than down here," I said, riskily.

"I know *that,*" Sandy said.

She looked down, touched my penis, and I was hard again. Then, curious, she bent forward so she could look at it. "Yours is big. Isn't it?"

How was it possible to do anything but grin. Wasn't she saying I was bigger than Gene? For a second I wanted to take Sandy by the shoulders and push her back down on the bed, but I was afraid she would think it was dangerous and I didn't want to be told no. I looked meaningfully at the clock. "Listen. Don't we have to get dressed?"

"I guess so. Damn. I wish we had more time."

"For what?"

Sandy got to her knees. She put her arms around me and squeezed me so tightly I was reminded that here was a girl who played Chopin three hours each day. She smiled lovingly, as if the whole conversation had never taken place. "So we could do it again," she said.

Three

24

Did I really love her?

That night, lying in my own bed, I returned to the question over and over again. The door to my room was closed; faintly through the floor I could hear the sound of the record player from downstairs, one of the records of Strauss waltzes that my father played endlessly, on nights when he stayed up to read.

Maybe I did! Wasn't it love when to hear her name sent a shot of adrenaline pumping through your chest? Wasn't it love when you wanted to call Alfred and tell him how wonderful she was even though you knew he might laugh and say you were "naïve"? Wasn't it love when you could be humiliated on the soccer field in front of a thousand scornful Jews, to leave the field knowing you had let down your own people and then, a few hours later, feel happy and clean as if you'd dribbled through three defenders and scored the winning goal? But as I lay there I couldn't help remembering what she had said about Gene Kleven, and now in a quiet bedroom, away from the distraction of Sandy's tits, I felt a surge of jealousy and hatred.

I *did* want her to be a virgin, whatever I had told myself.

I wanted to be able to hold her, look into eyes both frightened and trusting, and tell her how to do it ("It's gonna hurt, Sandy. But not much"). And here she was telling *me* what to do! And what about the weekends she had spent at Syracuse last winter? *This year!* I'd heard how they sneaked girls in. Was she giggling as she twisted herself through some open fraternity window? Whipping off dress and bra and panties, throwing them around the room and jumping under the blankets with Kleven, cuddling up against him because it was cold? Did she call herself a "slut" then?

It was black outside the window. I could hear branches rustle and dogs barking.

And now the miracle of no longer being a virgin couldn't obscure the fact that her talk with Kleven—and maybe her parents' divorce—had had something to do with it. I wanted to be liked for me, not because Sandy, a female Gatch, was looking desperately along the bench to find a substitute.

I wanted to call her up. In fact, briefly I thought about getting out of bed, walking downstairs to the phone, and dialing the number I knew by heart, not to yell at her: oh no. But just to ask her the questions turning around in my head.

But if I did I would probably get a sleeping Mrs. Bessinger ("Who? Whozat?"), wondering who was crazy enough to call her daughter at two in the morning, not to mention Sandy thinking the same thing.

Gradually I relaxed. After all, she had gone with Kleven for two years. And if I was jealous, that certainly wasn't her fault; I knew how wrong applying double standards was, and besides, what could Sandy have done that was any more reassuring than to take me home the way she did and lay me right in her French Provincial four-poster bed? As for

134

being a substitute, well, in soccer that's how careers started; why not here? I pulled the blanket over my shoulders, took one of the two pillows I usually kept under my head, and put it beside me.

Then I woke and it was morning. The branches that crowded against my bedroom window seemed especially leafy and green. Birds twittered. Through the branches the sky looked bright and blue. The pillow was on the floor. I felt too rested to be jealous.

I had done it!

And I would see her again! I would arrange it so summertime was a succession of mornings when I could wake late, knowing I didn't have to look at another geometry book as long as I lived. Mornings when my only responsibility was to call up Sandy, pick her up in the Chevy, and go across the Atlantic Beach Bridge to a golden beach where we could spend the day talking and chasing each other into the waves, diving into the breakers, then fucking all night on beaches, golf courses, behind tennis courts, and wherever else the Nassau County cops were kind enough to leave unpatrolled.

"Hercules vas stronger than you thought," my father said; he was always up first in the family no matter how late he read. Now he was dressed, sitting at the table and groping for his coffee cup without looking up from the *Times*.

For a second, a great stabbing rush of adrenaline went through me. He had heard about the penalty! Then I saw he was looking at a little box on the *Times* sports page. "They killed us," I said. "Why, the *Times* run something?"

"Just the score."

"Oh. Yeah, they killed us."

Gatch would have to discipline me. He would move me back to second team, and the thought of wearing one of

135

those torn red shirts when for a week I had worn the blue and white, the thought of coming off the field to sit on the bench while a triumphant Marshak took his place at left wing, was humiliating. It would be hard to tell Sandy. I'd get embarrassing questions from Alfred ("So you're on the bench again? I thought you were good").

○ ○ ○

By Tuesday, for the first time ever, I was thinking about cutting practice. I imagined parking the Chevy and walking out onto the field while Stein, Bruch, and the rest of the team looked up angrily, and Lupo and Gatch, whom I had let down, looked away. I imagined Gatch then coming over and putting his hand on my shoulder just the way he had done to Marshak and saying, "Son, it's back to the second team. You've got a lot of growing up to do."

But to stay home would have been so unusual my father would have begun to probe. That afternoon I came home from school, changed, and drove to practice. When I parked, Gatch, standing by the near goal with Lupo, gestured in my direction, which made Lupo turn around; then he walked across the parking lot to meet me.

"So," he said. "You think you disgraced yourself."

"Yes."

"Well, you're not far off. Pushing with the ref looking right at you. You cost us the game."

"I know," I said.

"Not that the rest of the game you played so wonderful. You must have lost the ball five times."

"I know that."

"It's so easy to pre*vent. Easy.* All you do, you screen the ball, move your body between the ball and him, and pass off. Don't you ever work on that?"

"He surprised me," I said.

"Well, he surprised a lot of people. *Theodoro* Christofila-kos," he said. "Milty's cousin. Also in their company. So don't feel so bad."

Relief flooded over me. "He's a pro?"

"Oh no. The family's too rich. They don't approve of their sons doing something so low, earning money from a game. But he was the best amateur around in Greece. He just came over this month."

"I wish I knew that Sunday."

"What difference would it make? You still don't push anybody in the penalty area."

Gatch was talking too energetically and enjoying himself too much for somebody about to fire a player. He turned around, walking toward the field, his hands jammed into the back pockets of a pair of old blue and white shorts. I caught up with him.

"I thought a lot about taking you off the team. Putting you back with the reserves," he said. "There's a lot of people on this team are hopping mad. Hoppink med, the way Bruch would put it."

I realized that, imitating Bruch, he was allying himself with me—someone else who spoke with no accent. I smiled.

"I tell them everybody's entitled to one mistake," he said.

"So I'm going to start."

"For the time being. But you're going to have to prove yourself each game."

"I'll try," I said. "Really."

Practice was awful. It wasn't that the team was unfriendly. Even Marshak said a grudging hello as I edged into a group passing the ball around. But nobody smiled at me either, and during the scrimmage, the kind of stage fright that usually

137

disappeared the first time I touched the ball hit me with Gatch's whistle and stayed until it was over. I had sense enough to see that I wasn't playing badly, and I was relieved that I was still on the first team. But I was sure they thought I was the weak link, the best they could get to replace a broken-down Marshak, so each time the ball came to me I felt on trial.

After practice, Gatch handed out copies of the league newsletter, which went to each player. I skimmed it, waiting in line at the water fountain.

The season was six weeks old. Hercules was in first place with a 7–0 record. We were in second, 6–1. The next team was Viking, 4–2–1—which in soccer was far behind.

"Ve beat Hercules negst time," Stein was saying to Bruch, behind me.

Bruch said something in Yiddish, which I understood to mean that that wasn't enough.

"Ef sher vellen die Vikings vinnen," Stein said.

"Ach," Bruch said. His tone said he didn't believe it.

I took my drink quickly and walked off, feeling alone. Most of the players were walking toward their cars in the parking lot. I turned to follow them.

By the goalposts nearest the parking lot, Marshak was struggling through some sit-ups, hands clasped behind his head, T-shirt pulled up above folds of stomach. He had played on second team. I had been so absorbed in my own play I didn't remember whether he had played well. Now he sat up, looking tired. For a second I exulted. But then Bruch and Stein jogged past me toward Marshak. Reaching down, Stein pulled Marshak to his feet. Then the three of them, in cleats, started on a slow jog, following the end lines around the field.

○ ○ ○

"You had a call from your girl friend," my mother said when I came into the house.

"*Mom.*"

Mom was standing in the kitchen, stirring something in a big pot on the stove. "Mm," she said, dipping a wooden spoon into the pot and tasting. "That's good. Isn't she your girl friend? Sandy Bessinger."

"We're going out. But she's not my girl friend," I said.

"Oh." She sounded surprised. "Does she have another beau?"

"Ma! People don't use those words." I laughed in what I hoped was a fair imitation of Ricky Nelson catching his mom in some impossibly dated bit of thirties slang. She couldn't know about Kleven! But such a burst of jealousy and rage shot through me, I had to walk out and upstairs, where I stayed in the shower until the hot water turned cool.

25

I had been careful not to tell Sandy I loved her. *Or* to ask her to wear my varsity jacket. *Or* to give her my class ring, which had arrived the week after the Prom, heavy in its velvet case. We didn't say it, but it was understood that for now we weren't dating anybody else and that we would see each other no more than three times a week, though we could talk on the phone. In case I had been tempted to go any further, Alfred was nice enough to give me a warning.

"Don't do it," he said. "Everybody feels like that the first

139

time they get a girl friend. Then two months later you want to go out with somebody new and here's this girl has your ring and your sweater and you can't even talk to anybody without her friends getting on the phone and telling her every move."

"Don't worry. I know that," I said, though I couldn't imagine wanting someone new. I hadn't told Alfred about getting laid. For one thing, I couldn't find a way to slip it into the conversation and not sound like I was bragging. Besides, I didn't want to embarrass him. If it looked like he was going to lecture me on sex, I changed the subject, proud of my generosity and feeling a little superior at the same time.

Actually, the reason I held off telling Sandy I loved her was this: I was afraid she would feel trapped by *me*. Wasn't she the veteran of a two-year romance with a college boy? Maybe she thought the mature thing was to let love ripen. I pictured myself saying, "Sandy, I love you," as we lay, tangled around each other in the backseat of the Chevy; she would stiffen, unable to answer, while I let the silence throw me into an agony of silence. If I said nothing, I wrecked nothing.

But I was beginning to think that I might, especially when we talked about my problems with the team, or her problems with Chopin, or the way we spent time with each other at school. That year Lawrence had moved into a new building, a low brick-and-steel affair surrounded by black asphalt parking lots and undeveloped fields, close enough to Idlewild so that every three minutes teachers would have to stop in midsentence while a jet roared overhead. As a reward for getting into Cornell my parents let me take the Chevy to school each morning. In the two weeks left between the Prom and

Regents' exams and graduation I would come in through the Lawrence parking lot gates, park, and walk toward the side door where Sandy, in a skirt and white blouse, was leaning against the wall or sitting on the steps leading into the cafeteria waiting for me.

To have a girl that I could be seen with! "Hi," I would say. "Got your history paper in?"

"Oh, God. That. No, I got an extension."

Except for history, where Mr. Brady took great pride in treating seniors like anyone else, there was almost no other schoolwork. Our days were taken up drowsing through final reports that didn't matter, leafing through the final issue of the *Mental Pabulum* ("Food for Thought"), named in the 1930s by a journalism teacher who was still there, having trained generations of "wordsmiths"; on afternoons that were warm enough, seniors took their cars and headed for the beach after lunch. It was a tradition even the teachers laughed at and kind of approved, joking about it to show us they were regular guys.

The yearbook was done and at the printers; still, we could get passes to sit in the Yearbook Office. "Meet you in Yearbook," Sandy would say. I would nod. During first study hall I would present my pass to Mrs. Gardner, who would smile wearily to show me she knew what was going on but take it and slip it inside her attendance book. I would walk through the door, saying hellos, pretending I was interested in the other kids, my heart leaping when Sandy came through the door. We couldn't talk much. There were other kids around. But by now everybody knew we had been to the Prom together and that we were "going out." When I sat down at the long work desk in the front part of the office, the other kids left the seat empty for Sandy.

141

At first we had lunch with Alfred and Barb. We would wolf down plates of ravioli in the cafeteria, then load up with Devil Dogs and head for the parking lot. To lean against cars, the metal hot from the sun, lick whip cream from our fingers, and talk! To feel, for the first time in my life, that while we talked, Mike Teutsch was sitting on the concrete steps behind the gym, wondering what it was that Howie Berger had done right! And afterward, when the bell rang, to walk slowly back in, Sandy talking a mile a minute, her head tilted up at me as if there weren't another person around!

26

I wasn't used to seeing what girls were like when you really got to know them; that is, when they weren't still trying to make you like them. I had thought of Sandy as shy, the kind of girl who, even though she could ask me to the Prom, had to use all her courage doing it, and who could cry because Mort Peskin made fun of her playing. Now I saw how confident she could be, especially when we talked about piano. She was becoming more and more interested in the idea of switching to pop piano, and one day, standing outside during lunch, she said, "I don't see why I can't be as good as Roger Williams."

"Sure. With a lot of work."

"I don't even think so much. He does a lot of things, they *sound* flashy. But nothing I can't do."

"What, you've been listening to the records?"

"And looking at his arrangements. He just doesn't sit down and play, you know. Everything is worked out and rehearsed, and for a composed piece they aren't so hard. They sound hard, all those runs in the top register. But they aren't *hard*. I know, that sounds kind of, I don't know. Arrogant."

The temptation was to say no. She was leaning against the car, arms folded across her chest, shaking her blond hair away from her eyes with a gesture that made me melt. It surprised me to hear myself say, "Kind of. If it was so easy, everybody would do it."

"That's true. Maybe there are things I don't know. But, God, Howie. It looks so easy."

I could see that arguing with her didn't bother her at all. In fact, she seemed to like it.

o   o   o

Four times in those weeks we went for a drive, and parked the Chevy by the Woodmere golf course; I took my blue blanket, the one that still had my name tag on it from my summer at Camp Ramah after fifth grade, and we cut through the bushes to some tree-lined fairway where I got laid. And the surprising thing was that it wasn't all fun.

"You sure you want to?" I asked the first night on the golf course.

"I figure we've done it, we might as well keep doing it," she said.

This was hardly enthusiasm. "I don't want it to be a favor."

"It's not." She hesitated. "I like it."

"You *say* you like it. It doesn't *sound* like you like it."

"Well, I can't say it doesn't bother me. But I like it a lot, too. I like it when you hold me."

"What about when I, you know, when I'm in you?"

143

"Howie, I *love* that."

"Because if that's a problem, we don't have to do it anymore."

"Howie, I *want* to."

But she jumped every time there was a noise in the scrub brush lining the fairway. She froze when the lights of some car turning onto Broadway flashed briefly across the trees above us, even when I was inside her and about to come. Afterward, she would sometimes become silent and look up at the stars, making me wonder whether Kleven was on her mind. At moments like that I would get a surge of jealousy so powerful I didn't know if I could keep it hidden. I had the strongest impulse to ask some innocent line of questions about him. And how had she done it before? And did they always use rubbers? Oh, very innocent. But I was afraid that if I started asking, before I knew it, I would be accusing her of liking him still, or of thinking about him, and then I wouldn't be able to control myself. I kept quiet.

Another thing. Each of the four times, she would get excited to a point. Then she would seem to relax and whisper, *"Do you want to finish off?"*

Had she had an orgasm? Whenever I tried to ask her, my tongue froze. But it seemed to me something that Kleven would know, and lying quietly on the blanket, looking up at the stars, I would feel ignorant, young, full of hatred, some of it even directed at Sandy, whose head was cradled protectively on my chest.

Who would have guessed sex was supposed to be tense? It was only when we were done and back in the car that we relaxed a little, because then I could put my arm around her and she liked that. She usually wanted food and so did I; that meant Nathan's, Nathan's of Oceanside, about twenty

144

minutes away by car, where, on a hot night, kids wearing varsity jackets or T-shirts and bermudas would hang around their cars or trade jokes with the cops who stood outside each exit.

Here was a place! Inside, people waited six deep on lines for hot dogs or thick, sweet french fries or clams. Sandy and I would head for the clam bar, waiting while the men behind the counter would reach into the shaved-ice bed, pull out a clam, then slice into it with a cutter that made a scraping sound like you made running a knife across a blackboard. Then we would take the soggy paper plates, heavy with clams, lemon wedges, and little cups of cocktail sauce, across the floor wet with spilled Coke or beer and sit at a table where we would let the clams slide down our throats and hold hands and watch for kids from Lawrence.

There I could convince myself everything was so wonderful that soon sex would be wonderful too, especially one night when, sitting with Bobby Baranoff and two kids from Hewlett, we saw Gloria Wondrofsky come through the tables with a large, tall man, dressed in bermuda shorts, tailoring his stride to hers as she dragged her leg across the floor.

"Look who's here," I said.

"Who? Oh, Gloria."

"The gimp," Baranoff said.

I laughed. But Sandy said, "Do you know her?" to Baranoff. "She's very nice."

"She is nice. True statement," I said quickly.

"GLORIA. HEY, GLOR," Sandy called. She waved Gloria over and, after getting their hot dogs, the two of them did come over. Sandy asked them to sit down and talked to Gloria like she was a friend, which made the man, who turned out to be her father, very happy. He turned out to be pretty nice himself; he said he had seen me play in a soccer game and proved it by remembering I had scored the winning goal.

"I was so glad you did that," I said to Sandy later, in the car.

"You didn't mind?" she said.

"Mind? I thought it was terrific. Really."

"In a way I was faking. But I felt guilty we made fun of her one time. Remember?"

I could see she actually felt virtuous. Well, didn't I?

"That was me," I said.

"No. We both did. But you were good today. You could talk to her father."

If I couldn't say I loved her, I didn't have to pretend I wasn't pleased. "Hey," I said. "You're really, uh, great. You know?"

Sandy looked sharply at me to see if I was kidding, then away, reaching forward to turn the knob on the radio to WQXR, the classical station. But she was smiling.

27

We had graduation on the football field. The day was sunny and hot; beneath our purple robes we were sweating. I stood with Sandy until the band began playing "Pomp and Circumstance" very slowly; then we smiled, Sandy blew me a kiss, and we separated—boys and girls were on opposite sides of the aisle so we could alternate while we went up to get our diplomas. Planes from Idlewild kept coming in low overhead, punctuating the speakers. Susan Rosenzweig, the first-honors speaker, saw her papers fly up in a gust of wind, tried to finish her speech from memory, stopped, and sat down. After diplomas were given out and we were dismissed, we let out an enormous whoop, threw caps in the air, and then spent a half hour deciding whose cap was whose because Mr. Cohn reminded us over the loudspeaker that caps had to be turned in and "checked *off*."

Alfred picked his way through knots of kids and around folding chairs toward me.

"Keep your robe on. My folks want to get some shots of us," he said.

We walked back the way he had come, toward the visitors' side of the stadium, where I saw his parents and grandparents waiting by the railing. Alfred's father was standing with his back to the sun reloading a big brown Polaroid.

Alfred was walking slowly. He wasn't smiling.

"What's on your mind?" I said.

"Nothing," he said. "Nothing. Except tonight I'm going to break up with Barb."

It struck me with surprise and pleasure—like the first time I had seen my father mishit a corner kick—that Alfred didn't exactly have things under control.

"Really?"

"We've been fighting for three months straight. All the time. Not to mention, Ellie's hot for my bod. I want to go out with her."

"But Barb's so great," I said.

It just slipped out. But Alfred had made up his mind. He didn't want to hear anything nice.

"I'm glad you think so," he said.

We came up to the fence. Alfred's father was smiling at us. We smiled back.

"Hey, here's the boy," said Alfred's father about me, setting the Polaroid distance gauge.

At that moment Barb came running up. "Hi, Mr. Lowey. Hi, Miz Lowey." She gave them both a hug, leaning over the fence to do it. Mr. Lowey took her around in the arm whose hand didn't hold the Polaroid. "Here's my favorite girl," he said. "Happy graduation. How about a couple pictures?"

"Oh, Dad," Alfred said.

"Alfie, it's okay," Barb said. I had never seen her so cheerful around the Loweys. It was as if she was appealing to them for help and at the same time sending him a message ("See? Your parents like me"). "How about one of the three of us?" Vamping a few steps as she came between Alfred and me, putting her arms around both of us.

"That's good," Mr. Lowey said. "Hold that. Let me set the gauge here."

We held the pose. Out of the corner of my eye I could see Barb look up at Alfred and give him a little extra squeeze around the waist. Alfred didn't move.

I was upset. But I was more upset later, when I described it to Sandy.

"Well, it happens," she said.

"No, but, Sandy. It was sad. I mean Alfred's my friend, but I feel bad for Barb."

"Oh, I know you think this is cruel," she said, sounding not only uninterested but impatient with me. "Believe me, a guy like that she's better off leaving."

148

28

I thought that was unfeeling. But that night there were about ten graduation parties. I picked up Sandy in the Chevy and we made the rounds, staying about a half hour at each, long enough to say hello, sign yearbooks, exchange information with kids we didn't know very well ("So where are you going? You going out of state?"), drink punch, and eat pretzels poured into crystal bowls that looked exactly the same from one finished basement to the next; it was so busy I couldn't reflect much on what she had said.

Sandy had to be home before midnight. Her father had taken an apartment in Glen Oaks, furnished. He had asked if she would stay at his apartment that night. He would come in from Glen Oaks to pick her up; the next day he wanted to take her down to Philadelphia to visit his relatives.

I might have been hurt by this—did she have to say yes on Graduation Day when by all rights we should stay out until morning, winding up on the golf course for an hour or two? But Sandy, in apologizing, had sounded as sorry as I was. Besides, the fact that we could enter a party as a couple and that people knew it ("Hey. Here's the lovebirds") filled me with love for Sandy, and that went double after Mike Ciparelli's party.

Usually Jewish kids and Italian kids didn't mix. The Italian parents were janitors, cops, or gardeners. In the summer the streets in Cedarhurst were filled with old dented green stake-bed trucks with mowers and clipping tools jumbled in the back and names like Ganitelli, Romano, or Rizzo on the outside: my parents' gardener was a Ciparelli, Mike's uncle.

When we came inside there were about twenty kids, all Italian. There were also some grown-ups; the party wasn't in the basement; people were holding wineglasses and were clustered around an ornate upright piano in the living room. We spent an awkward twenty minutes being introduced around by Mike, shaking hands with kids we had only seen in the halls during the four years of school, with girls who were taking jobs in banks and boys who were going into the Marines.

It was small talk filled with silence until, during one silence, Mike said, "You know, Sandy here, she's a great pianist."

He said this to his father, a small man with a red face, broken veins on his nose, and black hair, combed straight back, who had been seated on the piano bench when we had come in and had barely nodded to us. There was a rumble of agreement from the seniors standing around. Sandy blushed.

"Why don't you play us something?" said Mike.

"Oh no."

"Sure, why not?"

I thought she would play some of the Chuck Berry she had been working on, but she played "Autumn Leaves" instead. It was graduation; some of the kids here were going into the Army. Standing around the piano bench, girls reached for their boyfriends' hands or fingered class rings hanging from their necks. I thought of Alfred and Barb, and the practices I had been through with Mike, and how years from now we might not even remember each other's names—even *Sandy*, who had pushed me into going to the

150

Prom and shown me the new uses to which you could put a golf course—even *Sandy* might be thousands of miles away! When she was done, I saw that even Mike's father was looking straight down at the floor, wiping his eyes with a fist and wiping it on his hair.

29

"You were great. Great," I said when we were back in the car.

Sandy was excited. "That's the first time I ever did that in front of people."

We crossed Central Avenue, the street that divided the Italians from the Jews. The Italian streets had been lined with old frame houses that looked shabby even at night; the porch to the Ciparellis' house sloped and we'd had to step over a sagging board as we took the steps leading to his front door. Fashionable as it was to disparage our parents' houses—so bourgeois, after all—I liked being back in our neighborhood, driving past houses with fieldstone fronts and picture windows and little octagonal gaslights and plaster stableboys planted in the middle of carefully manicured front lawns.

Driving down dark streets, "Autumn Leaves" still running through my head, I could feel sentimental in a way that didn't seem quite right in a brightly lit living room. Two months ago I was wondering if I would ever touch a girl's breast—really touch it, nipple and all. Two months ago I would see Mike Ciparelli's girl friend slip an arm around him and have to turn away out of envy. Tonight, as Sandy had gotten up from the piano, Mike had started the applause and compliments ("Hey, that's nice, Sandy. Real nice") almost as if he had a crush on *her*. On my girl.

My girl! I had a girl! Suddenly I wanted to tell Sandy I loved her, and if Alfred thought that was a stupid thing to do, maybe he didn't know everything.

The trouble was, she sat leaning against the window, holding my hand, but saying little, appearing suddenly so tense I guessed she was thinking about her father and didn't want to be interrupted. I kept quiet. When we pulled into her driveway, the Cadillac wasn't there.

"He's late," I said.

"I know. Want to come in?"

"Sure."

Sandy's mother was in the living room when we came inside. She was sitting on the couch opposite the piano, wearing a dress and smoking a cigarette. She blew a stream of smoke into the air and dinched the cigarette into an ashtray on the coffee table.

"Pop's late," Sandy said.

"I know. Hello, Howard."

"When's he coming?"

"I'll tell you." She smiled.

"I'm just going to the bathroom," I said. Sandy nodded. She looked distracted. "Tell me what?" I heard her say.

But then I was walking down the hallway and into the downstairs bathroom. I was happy to be alone. There was something going on and I wished Sandy hadn't invited me in. I pissed. Then I flushed, waiting for it to be finished before washing my hands. I could hear the murmuring sound of their conversation through the door. There was a sudden rise and fall that sounded like Sandy. Then there was a lower sound: Mrs. Bessinger.

I couldn't stay in there forever. I came out, walked back down the hall, and was right on the verge of entering the living room when Sandy said "Oh, Mother. How could you?"

Mrs. Bessinger said something.

"But I'm *supposed* to say that," Sandy said. I slowed up, but Sandy had already looked up and seen me. "She told him I changed my mind."

"You said you preferred to stay here," Mrs. Bessinger said.

"Just because of the air conditioning. Oh, Mother, that's so *cruel* to him. How could you?"

"I'll be the judge of what's cruel. Cruel. I'll tell you cruel. I'll tell you what it's like to live with him for twenty years. That's cruel."

"I'm calling him."

"He hasn't got a phone yet. Look. San. Come to your senses."

Sandy broke into a long, high-pitched wail as if she wanted to cry out but couldn't, but couldn't stay silent either. It was a keening sound, her face twisted and her eyes closed, her arms held straight down at her sides, the fists clenched. Then she began sobbing. Mrs. Bessinger just watched her. Her legs were crossed and her ankle was working nervously. She lit another cigarette. "Sandy, I'm sorry—" she began once. But Sandy began sobbing again. Then she ran back through the living room, and out the door, slamming the screen door behind her, still crying so loudly I could hear her. I looked at Mrs. Bessinger. She looked at me. She sucked on the cigarette. I turned and followed, seeing Sandy just visible in the dark and catching up with her halfway down the drive.

153

"Sandy."

"Take me away from here. Take me away from this *house!*"

I was brought up to believe that you don't run out when your parents are talking, but this time I didn't object. We got in the car. "Where do you want to go?" I was looking toward the front door, expecting to see Mrs. Bessinger, but there was only the yellow glow through the screen and a glimpse of paintings from the opposite wall.

"Just away. Just away."

30

Her father had called earlier, about ten, just to say he would be there. Mrs. Bessinger had told him not to bother, that Sandy had been complaining about having to go.

"Were you?" I asked Sandy.

"No. *Never.* Oh, Howie."

"I thought you didn't get along with him."

"The night at your house."

"That. And the time about the movie."

"No, he was upset. We get along. But my *mother.* Making fun of him all the time. Telling him he was a lousy business-man. In front of me. Oh, Howie, she used to yell at him at the dinner table every night. He would just get quiet and more quiet. And oh . . . if he said he liked my playing, she just told him he didn't have any taste. Which he didn't, let's face it. Anyway, he didn't know much. But he admitted it. And the fights." She started to cry again, recovered, and went on. " 'You call yourself a man?' She used to say that

154

all the time. *'You call yourself a man?'* And also, you know what?"

"What?"

"But this is something you can't tell."

"Okay."

"I think she has a boyfriend." She lowered her voice, as if there might be someone listening on the roof.

"Oh," I said, embarrassed. "That's bad."

o o o

Later, at the golf course, the blanket spread out on the ground, both of us lying on the ground facing each other, elbows propped on the ground, cheeks supported by our palms, she seemed recovered enough for me to reach out a hand and run it down her arm.

She moved closer to me. "Should I just go over to his place?" she asked.

For some reason I wondered if she really wanted to ask my advice or whether she was pretending because she knew I would be flattered.

"I'll drive you."

"What time is it?" She held her arm up to let her watch catch the moonlight. "Oh. No, I guess not."

"Also, we don't have to, uh, do it tonight."

"What?"

"Well, just, we're here and whenever we're on the golf course we, um, do it"—I was stammering because never, in talking about sex, did we know what to call it. *Fuck* was too crude. *Making love* meant something I wasn't ready to say. *Going all the way* was too cumbersome—"but you're very upset and—"

"Oh, no. Oh, Howie. I want to."

"You do?"

"You've been so good to me tonight. I want to. I don't mean I'm doing it as a favor. I need it. I need you. Really."

I could have told her I loved her right then. I felt a tingling rush of warmth up my spine and neck. Suddenly, with a ferocity that matched her tone, she put her arms around me. She kissed my face and neck, her hands meanwhile pressing my back and the back of my head.

But what if this was all just a favor? What if the contempt she felt for herself about sleeping with boys ("I'm a slut") was temporarily being overwhelmed by her terror at being called a tease, a disappointment like she had been to her dad?

"Know what we could do?" she said.

I leaned back away from her, resting my elbow on the bristly blanket. "What?"

"We could do it without a safe."

"Oh, no. Sandy."

"I'm two days from my, you know. Monthly. We don't need it."

"Sandy—"

"Really. I'm very regular. We don't have to worry."

Through the blanket the ground felt hard and slightly cold. There was a warm breeze. There were crickets chirping. A few holes away we could hear the hissing sound of the automatic sprinklers. Beyond the high shrubs bordering West Broadway we could see streetlights and the lights of cars through the shrubs.

"You sure?"

Sandy nodded.

"Okay."

She was already on her feet, fumbling with the top buttons of her blouse. In a way, it was like losing my virginity again;

156

flesh to flesh, with no latex or lambskin in the way. When I was inside her it felt different; warmer, wetter, and whether that was what made the difference to Sandy I never knew, but suddenly she was moving harder against me and taking sharp little intakes of breath in a way she had never done before. Her eyes were closed until, as I came, she strained against me and sank down onto the ground again in little spasms that frightened and excited me at the same time.

"You had an orgasm," I said.

"God, did I," she said.

The sophisticated note in her voice stung, but I was careful not to let it show. "Was it a good one?"

She moved closer to me. In the moonlight her skin looked very white. There were goose bumps around her arms and thighs. "Can I tell you something?"

"Sure."

"I very rarely have them at all."

"Oh, Sandy," I said. "I love you."

"Women rarely do when they're younger," she said. "Except by masturbating."

Had I really said it? Had I completely lost my mind?

"Did you hear what I said?"

"Yes." Suddenly she was hugging me tightly, her face jammed into my chest as if she was afraid to look at me.

"Did I say it too soon?"

She shook her head.

"Because I could have said it earlier. I wanted to give you my letter sweater. I wanted to give you my ring. But if you think it's too soon I'll put them away. Until you say yes."

It was a lie. I would have hated her. But I didn't have to confront that possibility. She took her head away and looked at me. "No," she said. "I love you."

"Oh, I love you," I said. "I love you."

"I do, too," she was saying. "Really. I really do." She said it a few times, as if she wasn't sure if it was to convince me or her or both of us.

31

I had promised my father that the car would be in the garage by one o'clock, but that night we clung to each other, parked in front of her house, until a light went on in her mother's bedroom and a head poked through the curtain for a second before turning into a shadow.

"I guess I have to go in," Sandy said.

"I wish you didn't."

"Me too. I wish we could stay somewhere all night."

"Wouldn't that be great?" I said.

"I would love it," she said.

"I love *you*."

"I love you," she said and was out of the car.

I watched her go up the steps, hoping she would turn and smile at me one last time before putting a key in the lock. She did. On the strength of that I went home and jerked off twice.

The next morning I slept until my mother knocked on the door and said, "Eleven o'clock. Alfred's on the phone."

"I did it," Alfred said.

I hardly heard him. "I'm in love," I said.

"It really wasn't so bad," Alfred said. "She cried. I cried

too. But when I went home I felt so *happy*."

"And she loves *me*," I said.

"I'm in love, too, I think."

"Ellen Stern?"

"Naturally. When I got home I called her."

"I think you're making a big mistake," I said, more because I had planned to say it the night before than because it was on my mind.

32

For a while that month I was scared every morning when I woke up that she wouldn't answer the phone or that she would want to take a day off or that when, with people around, I reached to hold her hand she would be embarrassed. But when I got up the nerve to tell her that one day, she was smiling and nodding her head even before I finished.

"I know how you feel," she said.

"How?"

"Because that's the way I feel."

"Hey. That's exactly what I wanted you to say," I said.

"I know that, too," she said.

She had visited her father a few times. If there were tensions she took them out at the piano. In fact, now that school was out, she was practicing almost every spare minute. Whenever I came to her house I would hear the piano as I climbed the front steps, and as I rang the bell, I could see her through the living room window, hunched over the keyboard.

I had never realized how much practicing a pianist put

in. It made me a little uneasy—was I being a dilettante about soccer?—except that she was so unsure about her own skills and respectful of mine ("How can you do so much with your *feet*?"), I couldn't feel threatened. Though she would sometimes talk about how there was a "whole world" of music outside classical piano, the idea of giving up classical was painful to her. She had a group of friends, all classical musicians; once, when we went to hear one of them at a Young Artists Recital at Town Hall, I asked if he played pop, too.

"God, no. And don't you ask him."

"You mean he doesn't know about you?"

"Howie, he would die. And so would I."

So if she practiced six hours a day, four were reserved for Beethoven and Bach.

But there were stacks of pop books on the piano, brought home from the store. She got tired of playing rock and pop songs after a month; but one day she called me up and said, "Don't laugh at this. Could we go into Queens and see Liberace? He's playing at Forest Hills."

"Do you want to play like *him*?"

"Well, I don't want to *look* like him. But playing, I don't know. What's he like?"

"I never listened to him," I said.

We went. We sat in the top row of a stadium that had held tennis players that afternoon and watched him come out in gold lamé and sequined outfits that caused a rush of "Ohhhs" to run through the crowd.

Sandy laughed, but when he played she sat forward, looking and listening without moving. The next day when I came over to take her to Rockaway Playland there was a new stack of pop arrangement books on the piano—Roger Wil-

160

liams, Peter Duchin, and Peter Nero—and she was playing an arrangement of "Canadian Sunset" that sounded just like one we had heard the night before.

"Listen to that," her mother said to me; for some reason she thought of me as an ally. "A girl who could memorize the Two-Part Inventions when she was six."

It made me mad. "Two more years," I said, surprised at my nerve, "and she'll be selling out Forest Hills for concerts."

My parents had given me a graduation present and it was this: I could spend the summer without working. After graduation I had my days free and, except for her six hours a day at the piano, so did Sandy. It was the first year I spent any time at all in Manhattan. The first Saturday after graduation, we took the Long Island Railroad into Penn Station. There Sandy turned out to be a girl who knew the A train from the E train and the IRT from the IND. We took a subway to the Village, which to me was only an exotic hotbed of illicit drugs and beatniks. We walked, holding hands, down streets filled with shops and little restaurants; we bought ice cream from a Good Humor man and browsed through record stores and looked at weirdos.

Then we took a bus back up Fifth Avenue. We pushed through the revolving doors into the ground floor at Tiffany's and spent fifteen minutes looking down into glass cases filled with necklaces and pendants and ornate brooches made of clusters of emeralds and rubies and yellow and purple stones we couldn't name, until a saleslady came up and said, "Interested in anything?"—when we shook our heads and retreated through the doors as if we had been caught.

We walked into Central Park and watched some Africans play soccer. We walked through the zoo.

"You really know the city," I said.

"I'm in here all the time."

"You mean dates and stuff."

"No. *Howie*. With my mother. We go to concerts."

33

By the end of July, Hercules was 10–0–0, we were 9–1–0, the Vikings were still in third place at 6–2–2, and no other team was close. The message was clear. If anybody was going to beat Hercules it would have to be us. We would have to beat every other team, too; then in August, a few weeks before the season ended, beat Hercules, finish in a tie for first, and go into a play-off.

Of course, if the Vikings managed to beat Hercules we might win outright, but that wasn't likely. If the Vikings beat *us*, then Hercules went into the Nationals to play teams from Texas or California that could barely get into our league.

Game after game, we got better. We beat the French, 4–2. We went without scoring for seventy minutes, then scored three goals in fifteen minutes against the Vikings: 3–0. We beat the UN team, 3–1; I scored twice in that game. Afterward some of the players made a point of coming over and saying, "Niz game." But they weren't really any friendlier. They would talk to me. They might grudgingly compliment a pass if it was terrific. Some of the subs would crack jokes to me. But Stein, Bruch, and Levy never said a word.

And then there was an upset. The Vikings played their

second game against Hercules and won, 1–0.

I saw the game. It was a fluke; Hercules controlled the ball most of the game. They had twice as many shots as the Vikings, every one hitting the crossbar or going over the top. In the second half the Viking left inside took a long shot that glanced off a Hercules player's knee, head high, right in front of the goal, and right in front of Gunnar Elfsen, a tall, blond, awkward center forward whom the rest of the league laughed at because he was constantly tripping over himself, but who could head anything. After that came thirty minutes in which it seemed like eleven Viking players were on defense.

"We *beat* Hercules, we *win*! We tie, *they* win!" Gatch kept saying at the next practice, walking from player to player, in case there was anybody who hadn't figured it out on his own.

I thought maybe, united by a new purpose, the team might like me better. But I was wrong. That was clear the next day when we played against the team from Lufthansa.

It was a game played in almost total silence. In 1961 it was still possible that some forty-year-old Lufthansa mechanic had been standing guard at Bergen-Belsen in 1944. It was if hatred between the two teams was so total that to banter at all would have resulted in murder. In fact, when Lufthansa had been admitted to the federation, Maccabiah had threatened to withdraw. We had been outvoted—this had been two years before—and decided to stay in the league not only because it was the best league around but because Gatch had watched them play and was sure we could beat them, which we did, every time.

I have to admit it: I felt absolute hatred when I saw some

of them step on the field, these blond murderers and sons of murderers, these butchers of forty of my father's first cousins, laughing, talking in German, kicking a ball around with a repellent power and grace.

Actually, Lufthansa had a small office in New York and, aside from the first group, not many good players. In fact, there was an American named Reilly in goal. But that didn't matter. To us they were all Germans. It was our best game. In the second half, us ahead 1–0 and nervous that the score was so close, Yitzchak went up the middle and passed to Levy. Levy sent a perfect return pass on the ground, splitting two Lufthansa fullbacks. The American goalie came out. Yitzchak faked a shot. The goalie stopped short. Yitzchak swept the ball by him, past the near post and into the netting. Watching, I ran in like everybody else, pounding Yitzchak on the back, grabbing Levy's hand.

Afterward, Levy, Bruch, and Stein and the others took off for Segal's, leaving me sitting on the grass, changing into sneakers while cars filled with players and fans pulled out of the lot. As I walked toward my Chevy I saw that Yagoda and Yitzchak were bent over the hood of Yagoda's car, a gray 1953 Dodge whose backseat was always filled with paint cans and canvas furniture covers.

"What's wrong?"

"Broken water hose," Yagoda said.

"Need a lift? I can take you to a gas station."

"No. Ve leave it here. You know vere is Segal's? Is dot out de vay?"

The amazing thing was how weak and trembling I became. Did he mean I should come, too? "No. Just tell me which street. I mean, I know it's Rockville Centre. Just I don't know where."

He and Yitzchak got into the front seat.

"I really wanted to win that game," I said, overheartily, as we pulled out.

Yitzchak didn't say anything. He was looking out the window. In the last month I had heard him talk a little in English with Gatch, so I knew he could carry on a conversation, though in a very heavy accent. I thought maybe he hadn't understood me.

"Me too," Yagoda said.

"The Nazi bastards," I said.

No answer. Then Yagoda, as if he was trying to be polite, said, "Zey don't like losing to us."

We drove in silence after that, except when Yagoda had to point out a street. When we pulled up in front of Segal's, which turned out to be a bar like any other, with a blue neon sign and another blinking neon sign in the window that said HOT PLATES, they didn't invite me in. As they pushed the car door closed I heard Yitzchak say, "I vant a beer."

o   o   o

The week after that, Lupo came back. It was our second game against the French. Gatch benched Bogen, a skinny, pale man a little younger than the others, who never smiled and who played in a knitted yarmulka attached to his kinky hair with a bobby pin.

It was a disaster, or rather it would have been except that the French were so weak it didn't matter. Ten minutes into the game, Lupo was so winded he yelled something to Gatch in Yiddish, then switched positions with Yitzchak, moving to left halfback. He stayed there the rest of the game.

With me on left wing, that meant we worked together. It also meant I could see more clearly than anyone how out of shape he was. After a while he was just too tired to

165

go after the ball. He didn't tackle because he knew he couldn't recover if his man got by, and when the ball came to him he got rid of it right away, even when he didn't see an opening, because dribbling ten yards would have drained him completely.

At one point I watched him get rid of the ball by crossing it to Bruch, then slow to a walk. He was limping, and I realized Lupo had problems besides conditioning.

At half time I saw him go over to Gatch; the two of them talked in low voices, looking worried.

But he played the second half. We won anyway, 4–1. When the ref blew three short blasts on his whistle, ending the game, I walked off with him.

"Really hurts, huh," I said, jerking my thumb down at his foot.

"It doesn't hurt," he said with such anger in his voice that I wondered whether he ever had been friendly.

"Oh. Okay," I said, and walked on.

"One second. Vot you mean?"

"Just it looked like it hurt. You were limping."

"Not me. I vasn't limping."

"I'm not arguing," I said. By this time I wanted to get away. I walked ahead again.

"Berger."

"What?"

"Vait." Lupo walked a little more quickly to catch up. "Maybe a little," he said, in a softer voice.

"I'm not blind, you know."

"I didn't know it was noticeable. Vun vik. Vatch next game."

We had three easy games in a row, so I guess Gatch figured

166

it didn't matter. But in the next game Lupo was only a little better. He was slow going to the ball; he was out of shape and sometimes it looked like he was limping. I was happy he was back, though. Maybe Lupo didn't deserve to play; on the field he made a point to call out praise to me ("Good cross, Howie! Vay to go!"), and at half time he sat down next to me and started talking strategy as if I were the very best around.

Toward the end of July, we played a game at Riis Park, in the Rockaways, farther away than we usually went for games. I drove over alone, as usual. But after the game Sirulnick had to go into Manhattan. It turned out there were four cars for seventeen players.

"I'll take some guys back," I said to Gatch.

There was a silence, though a number of the players had heard.

"Ve don't vant kip you from you hot date," Marshak said, pronouncing it *det*.

"I'll go with you," Gatch said in an extra-nice tone.

"You goink to Voodmere," Lupo said. "You can take me to ze synagogue."

With the two of them, Gatch in the front, Lupo in the back, I drove out of the parking lot and found my way to Beach Channel Drive. We drove along Jamaica Bay, separated by the rail from the water. It was almost dark. There were still fishermen, with pails of bait at their feet, hunched over lines, curving poles set against the rail.

That Gatch and Lupo had wanted to go home with me was clearly a gesture to make up for Marshak's rudeness. Now the fact that no one was saying anything made it clear that we were all thinking about it.

167

"Why does he do that?" I asked. "Marshak. Why is he so angry at me?"

"It's not just you."

"That's what it sounds like."

"Well, he's had a terrible life."

"He's one of zem, came out from a camp," Lupo said. "Tvendy-six years old, veighed eighty pounds ven ze Allies came in."

"Do you know he fought at Warsaw?" Gatch said.

"No."

"You know what that was? The battle of the Warsaw Ghetto?"

"Course."

"His family was hiding in a little underground cave. Something their father built underneath the house. Stocked it with food and candles so when the Nazis came for them it would look like the house was deserted. But they found them. Maybe someone told. He doesn't know. Anyway, one day the SS came. They heard them traipsing around, the family heard them traipsing around, then the trapdoor pulled open. All these Nazis dropping down. Lou's father starting fighting, got clubbed in the head with a rifle butt. Killed. Then they lined them up. But one of the soldiers got hurt. 'Here's what we do to people who break the law,' the leader says. Sergeant. Lieutenant. Whatever. He takes a pistol out of his holster and shoots Marshak's sister in the head. Right in front of him. Nineteen forty-three. You were eating Gerber's peaches and your mother thought things were bad because she couldn't get nylon stockings."

If he was looking for an approach to make me sympathetic he had picked exactly the wrong one. "That's ridiculous,"

168

I said. "Probably fifty of my father's cousins died in the war. Probably the same goddamn way. And what about you? Where were you during all this? Planting goddamn cabbages in a victory garden?"

I took my eyes off the road long enough to see Gatch looking surprised. Then Lupo surprised me.

"Dat's right," he said. "Lou's a miserable person. It's nossing you do."

"Before the war he was the best soccer player in Warsaw. Jew or Pole. The best," Gatch said. "After the war it took him five years before he could even touch a ball. He lives alone. Guy had two years' college before the war. Now ask him if he wants a better job; he just shrugs. Gives you this with his shoulders."

"I read about people like him," I said. "All they want to do is stay alive."

"Sometimes," Gatch said. "He's tried committing suicide, twice in the last ten years." There was a shortness in his tone I read as annoyance with me, as if I had been flip about something serious.

"Oh," I said.

We drove on in silence again. We were driving east and here it was almost dark. The red and blue lights of some fishing boats twinkled in the bay. Gatch half turned and said something in Yiddish to Lupo.

"English," Lupo said. "Ve not hiding stuff from Howie."

o   o   o

They had to protect him! Here was a man who lived alone, content to mop floors and swab toilet bowls, taking satisfaction only in the few hours every day when he could work with a ball and remember the days when nobody in Warsaw

169

was better. Maybe it was sentimental, but to people obsessed with the way the Holocaust had wrecked lives, wasn't he a perfect symbol? Was it any wonder that when he was finally growing old they would gather around him to resist some punk who might put him on the bench?

"Does Marshak have any friends?" I asked.

"Sirulnick. Yagoda. Bruch and Stein," Gatch said. As he did I remembered that one day after a game, as soon as the horn blew, Marshak, Sirulnick, and Yagoda had trotted off the field to be surrounded by three women and a bunch of kids ranging from three to about twelve, all wearing shorts and yarmulkas, looking like refugees from some kibbutz.

"Dey take care of him," Lupo said. "Invite him to deener."

It was like looking at a geometry problem for an hour, then seeing it laid out in front of you, step by inevitable step! It wasn't me at all!

"You're all of a sudden very curious about him," Gatch said.

Perhaps I could have shared this insight with them, but I was embarrassed. It seemed like an intimate thing to talk about with grown-ups. "Not really," I said.

"Is it because he's playing better?"

Gatch was right; Marshak had kept up his running. He was skinnier. His moves were quicker. Where before he would have been gasping for breath, he could keep the ball for fifteen or twenty seconds, dribbling and faking, then come right back on defense. It scared me to hear Gatch mention it. I felt the need to show him it didn't matter.

"No. I can beat him," I said. Hearing my defensiveness, I was embarrassed, but Gatch didn't seem to mind.

"I know you can," he said.

170

34

One Saturday morning my father was sitting in the TV room at the little blond desk by the window that looked out onto the backyard. He hated to work at home. Whenever he sat there he was working on what my mother called "investments," or paying bills, and that was what he was doing when he called me in from the breakfast table where I was reading the *Post*.

The checkbook was in front of him on the blotter. He smiled when I came in. "This is a great source of pleasure to me," he said. He handed me a packet of forms and a cover letter that had come from Cornell a week before. "First payment. To vun of the best schools around."

"Yeah. With a soccer team, last year they were 2–6."

"And a med school with some of the best professors in de vorld. You're not still bothered by zat."

"Not really."

"At Cornell you can be a big shot. A star. How is it going for you, anyway? Soccer."

"Pretty good. You mean with Maccabiah? Pretty good."

"I want to see you play."

A rush went up my back. "Suit yourself," I said.

I was hoping he would argue with me, but he didn't even seem surprised. "I know you're angry because I never go. I can see how you feel. But in twenty years you'll think different. You'll be a doctor—or something else, doesn't have to be a *doctor*, for God's sakes, but something. Not a bum.

171

Not a broken-down janitor playing soccer like dese friends of yours you so proud of."

It was exactly what I had muttered to myself at practice, but hearing him say it made me want to defend them. "Being a janitor doesn't make you a bum. Maybe that's what your friends think at work, but it's not what I think."

"That's true. Very true. I'm sorry," he said. "I do your friends an injustice."

I watched to see if he was mocking me, but apparently he was serious.

"All I meant was," he said, "I want you to have a life where you're happy. No regrets. Well, everybody has regrets. But yours maybe won't be so big. I vant you should be a good player. I loved soccer. I loved watching you play."

"Well, you didn't have to stop."

"Maybe that was wrong. I admit it. I'd like to see you play."

Oh, how I wanted to smile and hug him and tell him I wanted that too!

But wasn't he just feeling good because I was going to the school he wanted? Did he think that a few sentences of apology could erase two years of punishment?

"I'll believe that when I see it," I said.

"I know," he said. He looked at me for a moment as if to drive home his point. Then, apology over, he looked down, picked up his pen, and signed the check.

On days when there was no Maccabiah practice, I got a group of the better kids from Lawrence to meet me at the high school a little after five and practice until seven. Usually we did drills. Sometimes we ran five-on-five scrimmages. I was better than anybody there, but at least I was touching the ball.

Sometimes in the morning I would just take the ball out to the field myself, set up obstacle courses, and dribble through them. One day I bought a cheap rubber ball. The junior high football field was bordered by a high brick wall; I set myself up thirty yards away and would take five kicks with each foot, moving back a few yards after each group until I couldn't hit the wall anymore. And oh yes. I did no juggling.

It wasn't a conscious decision. I didn't even realize I had stopped until one day when I came out to the field to see Dickie Grustein trying to flip the ball up on his instep. I walked the entire length of the field watching him as he rolled it up, tried to balance it, then kicked the ground in disgust when it rolled off and away.

"You'd be better off learning to dribble," I said.

"C'mon, Howie. That's your favorite trick."

"Yeah, well. It's a waste of time."

Dickie looked at me strangely and I realized I was echoing Lupo.

Dumb. But now I noticed it was no longer fun to juggle, and the few times I did, and saw the other kids looking at me admiringly, my attitude was that they couldn't know much, and I would ease the ball down on the ground and practice head feints.

For a month I had hardly seen Alfred. It was my doing. I felt awkward around Ellie, as if I was betraying Barb; it was such a childish emotion, though, I couldn't mention it to Alfred. He must have sensed it; he never brought her around and he had stopped dropping over again after dinner.

I felt at some point we would make up. Meanwhile, that left plenty of time for what I liked to do, which was come back to the house, take a quick shower, change into bermudas,

173

and call Sandy. For the first time since I was ten, something besides soccer dominated my thoughts.

Since graduation night, Sandy seemed much more relaxed about sex. It was as if she had come to a decision to enjoy herself, which was perfectly all right with me. In fact, without the tears and tension, I suddenly realized that sex was more than a status symbol. It was fun, especially when we found a place to go where there were no cars cruising by, no cops, and no bugs.

It was a little gazebo by the sixth hole of the golf course. It had been built for golfers who needed to duck in somewhere if it rained or wanted to sit down while they washed grass stains off their Spalding Dots. I had noticed it the summer before when I did some running, and I suggested it because, inside, the seats were cushioned with plastic pillows that slipped on and off the metal frame just like the pillows on our porch furniture. If we slipped them off and put them on the concrete floor we could have a surface every bit as soft as Sandy's four-poster bed.

For a while, as we walked to it across the fairways, Sandy was as nervous as ever. I was too, until, inside the gazebo, we slipped the cushions off and saw that there were enough of them to completely cover the floor, just as I had said. We spread the blanket over them, settled ourselves, and lay still for a few minutes listening to night sounds.

"It's good," she said finally.

"That's a relief."

By looking out through the sides, between the railing and roof, you could see stars. From this part of the golf course no part of the road was visible and there were no sprinklers going. Far beyond the course you could see blackness where marshes met the water. It was so quiet that when I said "Not bad," I whispered.

"Why are you whispering?"

"Why are *you* whispering?"

I hugged her and began unbuttoning her blouse.

o   o   o

Some afternoons we went to the beach. It was turning out to be a hot summer; even in June it had been warm enough to swim. Sandy's father had canceled his club membership when he left, and so each day around noon we would come into my parents' club lounge in bermudas and T-shirts, Sandy carrying a little plastic carrying case. We would sit around for a while with Jane Stern or Rita Schnall or Steve Rosenthal and anyone who wasn't working and could afford to be at the beach club at noon.

Then we would go out the wooden ramp leading to my parents' cabana, really a little shed with a door made of pine slats and a little canvas divider so men and women could have some privacy.

That was almost the best part: getting undressed together. We could do it only on weekdays when the crowd was light. But we would shut the door, slip out of our clothes, and hold each other. I would run my hands over her body, feeling her breasts, sometimes pressing myself so tightly against her that I thought she would cry out.

We would go out onto the beach, spread a blanket, turn on the Zenith AM–FM portable radio I had gotten as another graduation present, turn to WINS, and then Sandy would roll over on her stomach and say, "Do me."

I would cover her with suntan lotion, letting my fingers stray under the top of the pink two-piece suit she wore almost every day ("Howie!"). Then she would close her eyes. I would throw a football around with some of the guys, not very well because since I was eight I had given all my time to a game where you couldn't use your hands at all. We would swim, then start kissing, bodies warm from the sun and sand.

"I can't believe I'm doing this," I told her one day. We lay, side by side on our backs. Only our arms touched this time. My eyes were closed. I could see the sun through my eyelids.

"Lying on the beach?"

"No. All the things we do. Going out."

"Why?"

"Because two months ago, no, three. *Three* months ago I was lying at home every night wondering if I'd *ever* have a date."

"Oh. That. Well, you got over that all right."

"I *think*. I think I got over it."

"You think? Oh, brother. I got noos for yuh."

"What's that?"

"We're dating."

That made me laugh, but more to show her I could laugh at myself. "No. Seriously," I said. "I mean I was so *shy.*"

"I know. That was strange."

"Because boys are supposed to be tough?"

"No. Because you got seven twenties on your college boards and the best body of any boy on this beach."

She didn't move and didn't raise her voice. She said it as if it was a fact.

"I love you," I said.

This was something of a risk; lately when I said it I noticed she had been recoiling a little before responding, and I'd also noticed she wouldn't say it first. But this time there was no hesitation. "I love you," she said.

Relieved, I put an arm over hers so my elbow was just brushing her breast, and looked down along her almost naked body. And then I noticed that on her ankle she had the ankle bracelet.

It was clearly the same one. In the bright sun I could see the linked hearts, the little gold clasp, and the thin chain dangling off her sand-caked legs.

The first thing was to make sure I was acting normally. I let my hand splay out over her wrist and began stroking it.

"Sun's great," I said.

Idiot! Talking about the weather as if that wasn't a dead giveaway that I was making small talk!

"Mm," Sandy said.

Maybe nothing *was* wrong. She didn't know that I had been noticing the bracelet for a year or that a casual remark of hers to Barb had been relayed to me. Maybe she thought it was pretty.

"You think I'd still be shy?" I said. "I mean, calling somebody else?"

That startled her. "Somebody else?"

"I mean if we weren't going out. Not that I'd want to."

She was looking at me, her eyes open, squinting. "I don't know. Maybe you would."

"I won't. Not at all."

"Well, we'll see."

"What do you mean?"

By now I knew I had brought up the subject to test her. Clearly the appropriate thing was for her to be alarmed ("Why'd you bring that up? Do you want someone else? Secretly?"). But she didn't seem frightened at all. "We'll see

177

in the fall," she said. "When you're at Cornell and I'm at Juilliard."

"Maybe," I said too brightly, "that will make us like, I mean, love each other more."

"Absence makes the heart grow fonder?"

"Sort of."

"I think it makes people break up."

Suddenly I was no longer aware of the sun. "Is that what happened with Gene?"

For a few seconds there was no answer.

"Not exactly."

"What did happen?"

"A lot of things. He wanted to go out. But so did I."

"But who was first?"

"Howie."

"I just want to know."

"Well, gee whiz. Some things have to stay private, you know. A person can have some secrets, even from a lover."

And then she was on her feet, walking down the sand toward the water, brushing a little sand off one thigh, pausing to scratch one ankle with the pink-polished toe of her other foot.

There was something wrong here. But I went after her, swearing at myself and frightened. "I'm sorry," I said. "I didn't mean to pry."

"Yes you did."

"No. In fact, I'm glad you didn't tell me anything. I don't want to hear about your old boyfriends."

She laughed. "Yes you do. You want to hear that you're better."

"Oh, I don't know. I—"

"And you are."

"I love you," I said.

We were just at the water's edge. Sandy reached down and scooped a little water and flung it at my chest. "I love you," she said.

It was almost as if I had pulled it out of her, but I was so grateful she said it at all, I told myself not to be suspicious. We walked back up the beach to our blanket, me reaching for her hand, vowing not to bring up anything that smelled of jealousy. As we lay back down on the blanket I ran my hand down her legs and stopped, pretending to see the bracelet for the first time.

"Hey. Nice. What is that?"

"What? Oh, that? Something from my grandma. So juvenile. But I like it."

Four

35

Well, so what if she had lied to me! Sometimes you lied to spare people's feelings! But the next day I was forced to wonder about it again when I took an old ball down to the junior high to practice corner kicks and, as I pulled into the lot, saw the green MG parked by the basketball courts. There, alone on a hot day, dribbling and taking jump shots, was Kleven.

He was wearing black sneakers and white socks; his shirt was off and sweat had soaked his gray Syracuse gym shorts. At first I thought I shouldn't say hello. But if he turned and saw me as *I* turned away, wouldn't that demonstrate to him that he made me nervous? Sure it would. So I went through the mesh gates onto the court.

Was it my imagination or was *he* nervous when he gathered in a rebound with one octopus-like arm and, in turning, saw me? "Howie."

"Hi."

He recovered quickly enough. "Hey, what are you doing here? Oh. Practicing."

"Yeah. You home for a while?"

"Home for the summer. School's finished."

"You playing for them?" I asked.

"Playing Varsity? Nah. That's big time, Howie. I went out for Freshman. Got in some games. But the Varsity is all scholarship kids. All these Negro kids, eight feet tall. They dunk. They hit from twenty-five like nothing. The end of last year I sat down and figured it out. These guys are too good for me. Face it."

He said this quietly, as if talking to an equal, which made me realize again that I liked him. At the same time, I felt better. It was as if by not going out for Varsity he stopped being an athlete and I could feel superior to him. I tried not to show it. "Well," I said, "I hear that's a shit life, playing scholarship. They boss you around."

We talked for about five minutes. He mentioned Sandy only as I left ("Say hi to Sandy for me"), heading for the soccer field. It took me a while to realize that I was happy because of a simple thing: he had admitted that the "Negroes" at Syracuse were too good for him. One of the things that must have looked so exciting about Kleven to Sandy was seeing him dribble downcourt, the whole school chanting his name. Now that was over.

That night, after dinner, I sat out on the porch wondering about jealousy and how you handled it. Sandy had gone to visit her father. I had nothing to do. It was still light. From the living room window you could see the tops of the trees across the street, streaked with sun. I went into the television room and sat on the couch, flipping through *Newsday.* I was fifteen pages into the supermarket ads, my eyes closing, when the phone rang.

"Howard Berger, please."

"That's me."

184

"Howard Berger the soccer player?"

"Right. *Howie* Berger."

"Howie, okay. Howie, thiz Walter Perkins. From St. Louis University. I'm in New York this week. I'm wondering if I can get a chance to see you play."

If I thought any part of me had put aside soccer for good, a rush of goose bumps along my arms and up the back of my neck told me I was wrong.

"Well, yeah," I said. "I mean . . . I got some games coming up."

"Excellent. *Ex*cellent. Usually I get my boas from St. Louis. Local boas. But I'm here for vacation and I remembered your application. You have some mighty impressive clippings."

In all my fantasies about such a conversation I had never imagined Walter Perkins being a man with a southern accent. Soccer coaches were immigrants. They didn't say *boas* instead of *boys* and use expressions ("mighty impressive") out of John Wayne movies.

But then Walter Perkins showed me he knew his way around, John Wayne expressions or not.

"I'm playing tomorrow night," I said. "Usually we play on Sunday, but tomorrow's a make-up game. I'm on this summer league team I play for. Maccabiah."

"Good team," he said. "You'd be in the nationals every year if it wasn't for Hercules."

"That's who we're playing on Sunday. Hercules."

"Afternoon or evening?"

"Afternoon."

"Afternoon. Wehell, that would fit raht in. Better than tomorrow night, anyway."

"One thing," I said, to be honest, "I'm already accepted at Cornell."

"That ain't written in stone," he said.

○ ○ ○

Dad was outside on the front porch, watching the sprinklers throw a high wall of spray first to one side then the other of the front lawn. I came bursting through the front door. "Guess who called?"

"Who?"

I realized that this wasn't news that would make him happy, but I felt vindicated. "Walter Perkins, the guy from St. Louis," I said. "He wants to see me play."

My father surprised me by twisting around in the love seat, looking up.

"He called for that? He must think you got possibilities."

"He didn't think that last year."

"No. No, he probably did. But he couldn't see you so he let it go."

"Maybe."

"Well, good. Let him come, see what he's missing."

"It won't do me any good."

"So why didn't you tell him that?"

I hesitated. "Because. Just hoping for a miracle."

I was standing, looking down at my father. He had one foot on the coffee table.

"You still vant to go, don't you? You sink you're that good."

"Good enough to play for St. Louis. Yes. Sure."

"You've seen zem and you're sure."

"Two years ago I saw them. They aren't any better than Maccabiah."

"Yes they are."

186

"Well, maybe because they're in better shape. But in skills they aren't. Game sense they aren't."

"And you really sink it's worth going out there."

I nodded.

"I better come out and take this look at you pretty soon. When's your next game?"

"Tomorrow. We got a make-up game."

"I'll come."

"It's six o'clock."

"I'll try to leave work early. If some man from St. Louis can come see you, I can come from Cedarhurst."

I wasn't used to saying anything charged with affection to him, but I made myself look into my father's eyes. "I'd like that," I mumbled.

Which was why, the next night, Thursday night, when I drove over to Hempstead State Park for the game against the Vikings, I was wearing a uniform freshly laundered and inside my socks were the shin guards he always insisted I wear. I was in the Chevy; Dad would drive straight from work in the Caddy. "Maybe I get there a little late, but I'll catch the second half. Believe me," he had said.

I had had a twinge of disappointment—why not the whole game?—which I was sensible enough to dismiss. I parked, got out of the car, and clattered across the cement in my cleats. The stands were empty; there weren't many Vikings on Long Island. Out on the field the Viking players were juggling or passing the ball in triangles among themselves.

And then I noticed there were no Maccabiahs on the field. I looked around. Our players were clustered by one of the benches, some sitting, some standing.

At first I thought I was late and that we had finished warming up. But I remembered seeing the bank clock. If anything, I was early. I jogged across the field. I could see Gatch and Lupo, their backs to me, standing, arguing loudly in Yiddish with Sirulnick and Levy. Sirulnick, looking past the others, saw me. He gestured with his head.

"He's here," Levy said.

Gatch whirled around and I realized they had been talking about me. Everybody was on the sidelines because they were arguing.

"What's going on?"

Gatch strode over to me, putting an arm around my shoulder. "Don't be upset about this," he said. "They don't want you to play. They want Marshak back in."

"We should have done dis *long* time ago," Sirulnick shouted. "Dis a team for *men.*"

"Shut up, Sirulnick," Lupo said.

"Sirulnick's right," someone else said. Stein. Sitting on the ground, arms clasped around his knees. It made him look surprisingly young. "I'll say it. I ain't no chickenshit."

At first things refused to register. I looked at Sirulnick, at Levy, at Gatch. Everyone was looking at me like I was a Lufthansa fullback. Even Yitzchak, standing with his hands on his hips, looked angry.

"They won't take the field unless I put Marshak in your place," Gatch said. "I told them we forfeit the game if we don't play. They say tough."

"Oh."

Marshak was lying on his side, pulling blades of grass from the ground. He was skinnier; even on his side his stomach looked flat.

"How can they do this? I outplay him every time."

"That was weeks ago, Berger," Stein said.

188

How many secret meetings had gone on while they plotted this? Were even the few players who talked to me at practice in on it? Were even they saying mean things about me? I turned to Gatch. "Put me against him next practice. I'll take him on one on one."

He shook his head. "This isn't the pros," he said. "I can't fire these guys. Something like this, everybody in on it together, I can't ignore it."

And at that moment, behind him, I saw a white Caddy pulling into the lot. Was it him? All I could see from a hundred yards away was a blur of face, but on top of the face was a hat. He had taken off early. I felt betrayed. "Where I come from," I said, "players listen to the coach."

"What?" Gatch said.

"Berger. Go take dot hot car back to the Five Towns," Sirulnick said.

"Vot he say?" said Yitzchak, motioning with his head toward me.

Sirulnick translated what I had said into Yiddish. There was some laughter and groans. Behind Gatch I could see my father swing his car into a parking space. He opened the car door and got out, stretching. He was still in his gray suit. He took off his hat and flipped it through the window into the backseat. I saw him look across the field. He slipped out of his jacket and loosened his tie, then began to walk toward the field.

"You can't take me out. You can't."

"Why not?" Gatch was trying to ignore the fact that I had insulted him.

"*Lots* of reasons. My *dad's* coming to see me. He's here now."

189

Some of the players actually laughed.

At that moment Lupo jumped in. "Berger should play," he said. "Marshak, if you had guts you'd quit years ago, I don't care how skinny you got."

Normally I would have been grateful. But it struck me that even if Marshak was playing like a pro, I should still play. *Lupo* should be on the bench. In the last week he had been no better and he didn't even bother concealing his limp. Dad waved at me. I pretended not to see. I turned my eyes on Gatch, who was in uniform, fingering the heavy whistle hanging from a blue and white lanyard circling his neck. At first I thought I had a chance. Gatch's lips were closed, but curved into a smile of sympathy.

"I had to outplay him to make starting team," I said.

"I been outplaying you," Marshak said. "I don't foul nobody in the penalty area, the ref looking right at me."

"That's *weeks* ago."

"It's nothing personal, Berger," said Bruch, the compromiser. "Ve got notink against you. Ve play better vit Marshak."

"How do you *know?*"

"Maybe we alternate them," Gatch said. "Play Lou one half, the kid the next half."

"Aaron, zis not the UN," said Sirulnick. "Zis is vat ve vant. Sorry."

Gatch looked at Lupo. Lupo shrugged. Gatch took a minute to look around at the faces of the rest of the players. Then he turned back to me.

"Howie, I'm over a barrel," he said. "This isn't the pros. I can't fire them. If they don't go on the field I don't got a team. Don't *have* a team. I work for them. They don't work for me. So Marshak's in."

190

36

My father was sitting in the last bench of the bleachers, by himself, removing cuff links from his white shirt, folding the cuffs neatly halfway up to a surprisingly white forearm, when I walked up to him.

"Better get out there," he said, gesturing toward the field, where the teams were taking positions.

"I've been benched."

"Tell me later."

I realized he didn't know what the expression meant. "Benched," I said. "I'll sit on the bench. Marshak—that's the guy out there, he's taking my place."

I half expected him to shrug and tell me that was the breaks. Instead he looked concerned. "Ooh. Dat hurts," he said. And that did it. Suddenly I felt I was allowed to cry. My throat swelled up. Tears began sliding down my cheeks. I knew the five or ten fans also on the bleachers could see me. I didn't care; I took the last few steps and sat beside him, hiccuping and gasping and wiping my cheeks with my hands.

"What is it? Howie. What is it?" my father said. He reached out, hesitated as if embarrassed, then put his arm around me. With a moan I sank my head in against his shirt, not minding the mingled odors of starch and sweat.

"They h-h-*hate* me," I wailed.

"Who does?"

I began to cry again. "All of them."

191

"The team? You mean ze team?" His accent thickened.

"They never talk to me. They make like I don't exist. They don't even think I'm a *Jew!*"

"Vait. Slow down. Vun sing at a time. Who doesn't like you?"

He had to wait until I was through sobbing. Then I told him.

"Every time I go out there it's horrible. They don't talk to me. After practice everybody goes to this . . . restaurant. They never invite me. But I don't care about that. Really. I'm better than half the guys out there. Okay, maybe not half but four of them. Better than Marshak, better than Lupo, he's the guy at center half. Good ball player, but his leg is bothering him. He can't outplay me on one leg. But that's okay, he's been nice to me. Him and Gatch. But the team, they just want Marshak in, and I came up to them today and they told Gatch they wouldn't play unless he put Marshak in, so he did."

I began crying again, the kind of mewing sound I remembered hearing from Barb the day I had gone over her house.

"Vell. Not a good sichation," my father said.

There was a reserve in his voice which told me that while he wouldn't argue, he might not believe this was all of it.

"It's true," I said.

"Oh, I can believe it."

"You can?"

"Sure. A rich kid from the Five Towns, playing with a bunch of Russians who had to leaf the old country and never had a chance to put their lifes togezzer."

"They're good."

"Listen to him. Defending zem already. Sure. Zey're good.

But I know zese guys. I used to go to zese games. They vouldn't like me either."

"They don't like German Jews."

"Maybe."

"Do you believe me?"

He smiled. "I'm not around, so I can't say. But you got a good head on your shoulders. If you say it, it's probably true."

○ ○ ○

It would be nice to write that things were now perfect between us; that I moved closer to him, comforted by his arm around my shoulders as the whistle blew and I watched a slim Marshak take the pass from Lupo.

Actually, my father took his arm back and sat, hunched forward, face in his hands, watching. "Good team. I forgot how good dese guys are." Five minutes after that, when Marshak trapped a ball and moved it downfield with a nice pass to Stein, he said, "Not bad. Say this much, he's not bad, zat Marshak."

How could anyone be comforted by someone so scrupulously fair? I tried to calm myself by thinking of what I could do next, but that was hard because soon I realized that, in addition to the humiliation of being on the bench, I had Perkins to think about. I didn't even know where he was staying. I could call St. Louis and find some way to track him down, but then I would have to call him to say I wasn't playing, and that was a prospect which made my face flush and drops of sweat trickle from my armpits down my ribs.

"I want to go home," I said.

My father looked alarmed. "That's not a good idea."

"They don't want me. I don't need them."

"Howie, zis your team. Maybe you don't all the time agree with your coach, but he's your coach."

"He's not much of a coach," I said. I stood up and walked down from bleacher to bleacher toward the parking lot. There, I turned to see he had stood as well. And, in his big white Cadillac, he followed me home.

37

She wasn't home when I called and didn't call back until eight.

"Let's go to Nathan's," I said.

"Okay. Something wrong?"

"I'll tell you later," I said.

On the drive out I was cheerful. I was saving the story for Nathan's, where, surrounded by people and fluorescent lights, it was less likely that I would cry. I knew it was all right with Sandy if I cried, but I wanted to talk about it in a sensible way, a boy who could laugh and joke and eat cherrystone clams even when he hurt. So I made small talk, telling her how good-looking she was and how much my parents liked her the times she had come over the house. The only trouble was that from the moment I first kissed her in the car she had acted strange.

It was almost as if *she* was upset. She had kissed me quickly and, instead of resting a hand on my thigh the way she usually did, kept bringing her hand to her mouth to clip off a hangnail, but then dropping it into her lap, leaving me to reach for it again. On line at the clam bar, her conversation kept fading out. When we sat down I noticed she had clam sauce, but no lemon. I stood up to go back.

"Oh, that's okay," Sandy said.

"You always get lemon."

"Sit down. I got some good news."

The unsmiling way she said "good news" made it clear that something was complicated about it. Sandy reached over, took a clam, speared it with a fork, pulled the meat free from the shell, and dipped it in the clam sauce. "I have a chance for a restaurant job."

"Great. Hey, great. What kind?"

"It's an audition. I play for two nights. If he likes me he takes me. I get paid for the audition, actually. Fifty dollars a night."

"Where is it? How did you get it?"

Sandy was looking down, stirring the ice around in her Coke with the straw. "Well," she said. "It's at Kleven's."

It was a good thing she was looking down. It gave me a second to recover from the unsettling jolt that hit my stomach.

"Oh," I said. I made myself keep smiling. "How'd you get it? I mean, did you run into him or something?"

"I called him up. Why not? He's got the best restaurant in town. He gets the kind of people who like to listen to the stuff. Yesterday I went down there and played for him and he said, listen to this, he said, 'Sandy, I didn't know you could play this stuff. This is fine.' "

"That's great," I said again.

"You don't mind, do you?"

"Mind what?"

"Well, I know you sometimes get bothered by stuff, involving, you know. The Klevens."

195

"Oh, that. Listen. I'm not saying there never was any of that. Jealousy of Gene, sure. But this. This is a great opportunity."

"You sure?"

"Sure I'm sure. Maybe you won't even need a scholarship, fifty bucks a night. *Jeez.*"

"I mean about Gene. Are you sure about that?"

"Absolutely."

"I can understand it. It's a natural impulse."

"*Sandy!* Stop worrying about something that doesn't exist."

"Okay."

"Not that it didn't exist. There were times I was jealous of him. But not now. It went away."

"I just wanted to be sure."

"Now you're sure."

"Okay."

"Okay. You'll have to tell me everything about it."

She looked hurt. "Oh, Howie. I want you to come."

Did she really think I wanted to sit at some back table, sweating in a tie and jacket, and watch fat Mr. Kleven come over and put a hand on her neck, smiling down at her like she was back in the family? But to say that would have been to confess that none of the things I had been saying to her were true. To say that would have been to sound like exactly the kind of jealous boyfriend she thought I was.

"Then I'll go. Sure."

"Oh, great. Great. How was the game?"

For the first time in a few minutes I remembered that I had something to tell her. I tried to recapture the mood I was in an hour before. But now I didn't feel we were equals. Here she was playing for the richest people in the Five Towns.

196

Was there any way I could tell her about the afternoon and keep her respect?

And that troubled me. If I loved Sandy and she loved me, I should be able to tell her *anything* without losing her respect.

Besides, two people couldn't always be equal! If the other person had a success you should be happy for her. The right thing was to be excited about her playing at Kleven's! The right thing was to tell her about how I was benched and how awful I felt and take comfort in the way her forehead crinkled up with concern.

But I didn't have the slightest interest in seeing her sympathetic. It would have mortified me. Looking past her to the clam bar, I saw some kids in Lawrence jackets stuffing money back in the pockets of their black chinos. They weren't kids we knew well, but when they turned around, balancing their Cokes and clam bar platters on plastic trays, I waved at them. "Not bad," I said. "Hey. Look who's here."

38

Maybe she would need me to make suggestions about just what kinds of music the Kleven's crowd would want to hear. Maybe she would be scared and clutch my hand as we walked up to the door of the restaurant, turning to me, her face white, and saying, "I don't want to go in."

But Thursday night, when I picked her up, I saw right from the first that things wouldn't happen that way. She had her music picked out; she didn't look pale at all, even in the black dress with a kind of scoop neck she had worn to Mike Ciparelli's party. She looked tan and she had used a kind of green eyeshadow that made her look sophisticated, like a college girl.

If you could see Nathan's a mile away, you didn't see this restaurant until you were under the awning, where a little wooden sign with *Kleven's* written in script was imbedded in the oak door. When I took her hand in the parking lot, she gave it a little squeeze and dropped it. "I don't think that would look cool," she said.

Cool! Since when did she use that kind of hip musicians' language?

"You nervous?"

"Yes." She nodded a few times.

"I'd like to hold you," I said.

"I wish you could."

"Maybe afterward we can go out to the golf course. Spend a couple hours at the gazebo."

For a second I thought saying that might make her angry. But she nodded again. "Yeah."

If it all seemed a little automatic on her part, I set it down to nervousness; anyway, it was unworthy of me to care at such a crucial moment in her life. We walked through the door, past a bar and a lounge area with tables and black plastic swivel chairs. Sandy went up to the bartender and asked for Mr. Kleven, who came bustling out, smiling, and put one big arm around her.

"Mr. Kleven," Sandy said. "This is my friend. Howie Berger. Mr. Kleven."

Even up close he looked nothing like Gene. He was fat, with a fringe of hair around his bald head. He was wearing a brown jacket and white-and-brown-checked pants and looked thoroughly the way somebody in this business should look.

"Pleased to meetcha. You here to listen? Just sit at one of the tables, we'll get you a Coke or something. Let me show you the piano."

I didn't get a chance to say another word to Sandy. Mr. Kleven swept her through the restaurant, introducing her to bartenders and waiters and ushering her to a black upright piano which sat in a little alcove, closer to the bar than the dining room. For a few minutes the two of them busied themselves, adjusting a light on the music rack, pushing the piano here and there; then he leaned over to speak into the little microphone set beside the piano.

"Ladies and gennulmen, uh, have your attention. Kleven's is proud to present a little something new tonight. Something for your enjoyment and, uh, listening pleasure. At the piano for the first time ever"—he looked over at Sandy and smiled at her; she smiled back—"first time ever in the Five Towns, Sandy Bessinger at the piano."

He moved out of the way. Sandy sat down to a little applause, mostly from people sitting at the bar. In the dining room people were eating and talking as if there had been no announcement at all. I saw Sandy looking over at them as if that would quiet them down. Then she went into "Autumn Leaves."

By this time I had heard her play "Autumn Leaves" so many times I could tell when she was making mistakes, and there were a couple but only at the beginning. But by the time she was halfway through, the playing was stronger and she seemed lost in it. She went into "Begin the Beguine," and when she finished, the crowd, at the bar and in the dining room, startled her by breaking into applause.

"Another Coke?"

I looked up. It was Mr. Kleven.

"No thank you."

He sat down. He was breathing hard as if he had just been running. There were beads of sweat on the freckled top of his head. He took the sleeve of his coat and ran it over his head. "She's good," he said.

"I know," I said. Sandy was grinning over at the people in the bar, one of whom had said something to her. She flashed a quick look over in our direction. Then she played a few chords and went into the medley of fifties songs.

"Well, this," Mr. Kleven said. "I don't know about this. This is for you people. Teenagers."

Looking around, I could see he was right. In the dining room there were a few people under twenty, but they were all with their parents or grandparents. Most of the tables were filled with people my parents' age in groups of four or six: Five Towns couples, the women with plunging necklines exposing the sun-tanned tops of breasts, the men in gray silk shantung suits.

"————" Mr. Kleven said.

"What?"

"I said, what song is that?"

" 'Graduation Day,' " I said.

"Graduation Day. Most of my customers, they don't even remember graduation day."

I didn't say anything.

"But she's good," he said. "I love her. She's like one of my family. Well, gotta go."

When Sandy took a break a half hour later and came over to the table, I made myself smile at her. She was flushed.

200

She sat down, reached over, and drained half of my Coke in three ladylike gulps.

"How'd I do?" she said.

"Fine."

Which was true. The tip-off was that people coming out from the dining room would stop and watch her before paying the check. "Kid's good," they would mutter, just like kids did when I had juggled in the gym after school.

"Nobody listens," she said. "I never realized that."

"What do you mean?"

"They go on eating and talking. It's hard to get used to that. It isn't like classical."

"They're listening."

"They are?"

"A lot of them."

"I guess I just hear the talking."

"Well, some of them, you're not playing their songs."

"Playing their songs? What do *you* mean?"

"These are all old people. You're playing songs we like."

" 'Begin the Beguine'?"

" 'Graduation Day.' "

I could see she was hurt. "But that was only about ten minutes."

"Well, that's what Mr. Kleven told me."

"Oh."

"I mean, he liked it. He just said that one group. The one medley."

"Did he say anything else?"

"Sure. That you were good."

And maybe I would have had a chance to make it up to her, except that just then she looked past me and I turned

201

around and there was Gene Kleven coming through the door. He was dressed in a jacket and pants and no tie. His crew cut was pushed up straight and he had a tan. He looked infinitely older than he had on the basketball court, much happier, and not surprised to see Sandy at all.

"Dad said you were doing this," he said. He actually had the nerve to give her a kiss on the cheek.

She shot a nervous little glance at me. "When did you get in?" she asked to make it clear this wasn't planned.

"This week. We—" He motioned to me. "We ran into each other on Monday."

"Oh." She turned to me. "You didn't say anything."

"I forgot," I said.

"How long are you home for?"

He sat down and stretched out his legs in the aisle. "I'm home for good," he said.

"Until September?"

"Until who knows. I'm transferring. Transferring to Hofstra."

"You are?"

It was as if I weren't there. He looked at her and she looked at him, and if he had added *and I want to start going out with you again* it couldn't have been plainer.

There was nothing for me to do except pretend I didn't see it. And now Mr. Kleven came over again with another man at his side. This man was younger, with black hair slicked back, wearing a black suit with a purple shirt and white tie. Mr. Kleven was laughing and joking with him and punched him in the elbow in a playful way as they came up to the table.

"Son. Al, you know my boy. My boy, Gene. Sandy, that

was very good. Better than I expected. Listen, Sandy, this is Al Perrino. Al, this is the kid you been listening to. Sandy, Al here is the owner of Luigi's."

Sandy suddenly became serious. So did I. Luigi's was the classiest Italian restaurant in Lawrence, and it had a piano, too.

"You're very good," Perrino said to her. "How much material do you have?"

"What do you mean?"

"In minutes. How much can you play without repeating yourself? I know you're new at this."

"An hour and a half."

"Fine. Tell you why. I need a replacement for my pianist. He's good, but he wants off another night a week. You do his kind of stuff. Fact is, you're better. He knows more material but you got better chops. Anyway, I'd like to try you. Fifty dollars a night. Thursday nights, nine to two. Howzat sound?"

Sandy was so excited she could only nod.

Perrino snaked a hand into his back pocket. He pulled out his wallet, extracted a business card, and handed it to her. "I don't want to bother you now. Call me tomorrow afternoon. Call at the place." He left, with Mr. Kleven leading him, one hand tugging Perrino's elbow.

"This is unbelievable," Sandy said.

Gene kind of chuckled. "Leave it to my dad," he said. "He knew Al was looking for somebody."

Could anything be more obvious? For a second I hoped Sandy would shrug her shoulders as if it didn't impress her that this clown was using his father to impress her.

That was all she would have had to do. Shrug. Catch my

203

eye. Give me a look that said, "Don't worry about this asshole. I know what he's up to."

Instead, she started shaking her head back and forth. "Your father," she said. "He's an amazing man. Amazing."

Gene stood up. "I'm going home," he said. "When do you get off?"

"I'm playing till eleven."

"Because the thing is, I could come back and Dad could feed us around eleven." He turned to me. "I mean all three of us. Three big steaks from the kitchen."

"Well—" I said.

"Great. We'd love to," Sandy said.

"See you later, then," Gene said. He left.

Sandy turned to me. "God. This is a miracle."

"I thought we were going to the gazebo," I said.

"Oh, Howie. Another night. This is a big night for me."

"I know that."

"I don't want to just walk out, all his father's doing for me. Did you hear what Mr. Perrino *said*?"

"I'm not deaf."

"Besides, I haven't seen Gene in a long time," she said. She was still smiling. "Can't I yak with him for a half hour without getting you all bothered?"

If she hadn't used a word like *bothered* I might have let it go by. As it was I stood up.

"Sure you can," I said. "You can talk to him all you want. I'm going home."

I said it to test her. That was why I stood at the table looking down at her for a long instant. I could hear the clink of dishes behind me. A group laughed uproariously at one of the tables in the lounge. A waitress brushed by me carrying a tray of salads. I was sweating in my wool jacket.

And I can still see her smile fading as she realized things were serious.

"Howie, this is my big *chance*. My big *night*. Why are you spoiling things for me?"

"I'm not. *You* are."

"You are. I was worrying about this all year. I thought you cared."

"Sandy, you were kissing his ass."

"What do you mean?"

She was happy. For one second, seeing her face aglow, her eyes wide, I thought I shouldn't spoil things for her. But I was too hurt.

" *'He's an amazing man. Amazing,'* " I said, mimicking her.

Her eyes filled up. She looked at me in an angry way that made me feel small.

"Why don't you just leave?" she said.

39

It was a comfort to see the Chevy sitting in the parking lot. It was a comfort to slide behind the steering wheel and turn the key, feeling the engine roar to life, and to steer the car out of the driveway into the street. It was dark. I turned onto Cedarhurst Avenue.

Was it over? Was this the way kids broke up—two people saying things they didn't mean and then afraid to take them back because they'd look dumb? Or maybe she did want me to go. Maybe she was happy I had left, so she could sit down with Gene when he came back and talk over old times.

Or had I made something out of nothing? How would I have liked it if she had come up to the bench during a soccer game and started a fight? Wouldn't I have told her to get lost? Wasn't this exactly the kind of jealous rage Alfred had warned me about?

I don't remember where I drove. I don't even know if I stopped for stop signs. I remember at one point finding that I was in front of our house, pulling into the driveway and getting out from behind the wheel. The back of my shirt was soaked with sweat. My legs felt weak the way they felt when I had the flu.

My parents were in the living room, reading. I made up something about Sandy doing "real well," which sounded like there was nothing at all wrong, went into the television room, and flicked on the set, but concentrating was impossible. Fifteen minutes later I flicked it off. I strode out through the front door to go for a walk. A block later I decided it was too hot and turned around. Back in the house, I looked through the bookcases, pulling out books, flipping through them, then snapping them shut and piling them on their sides on the shelves, too impatient to find the place where they had been, until my father, who since Tuesday's game had treated me with great care, looked up from his book and said, "Vat's wrong? Got ants in your pants?"

"No."

Maybe I should drive back to Kleven's. She was still there.

206

I could walk in, sit down at the table I had left, and apologize for being an idiot.

I was as paralyzed as I had always been trying to call up girls. I was so afraid she would laugh at me, or worse, lash into me for spoiling her big moment—which I had! I had spoiled it!—that I couldn't move.

Well, maybe she would call *me*! Maybe she would realize that it was dumbness that had made me walk out. The wild exhilaration of realizing this might be possible sent me out to the screened-in porch, where I sat waiting in the dark, looking up at the headlights of each car turning onto Prospect until it passed by.

Now my panic began to be replaced with anger. She knew the Hercules game was tomorrow. True, she didn't know I would be on the bench for it; shouldn't she make some allowances for how I felt? Wasn't that what someone in love with you was supposed to feel?

But the moment I examined that idea it fell apart. It didn't matter in the face of the possibility that I would lose her. Late as it was, I should call her, even at the risk of waking her mother, even with the humiliation of admitting how terrified I was, just to get her to say she loved me.

I tried to make myself stand up and go inside to the phone. Only as I did, a car turned in, the headlights lighting up lawns across the street for an instant. It slowed as it passed out house, then pulled over to the curb. It was Alfred.

The car door slammed. He came around the Plymouth and up the front steps, peering through the screen door to make sure it was me.

As soon as he did, I saw how at once naïve and stubborn it was for us to have avoided each other, and was so grateful that he had turned up it was all I could do to keep my

207

voice casual. "Hey, look who's here," I said.

Alfred pushed the screen door open and came inside. "Yeah, long time no see. Isn't that dumb?"

"Yes."

He sat. "Real dumb. Was it my fault?"

"I—"

"I don't think it was. You stopped calling right after graduation. Also, I drive by here a lot to see if you're out here, which you never are. Never. Let me see if I can guess." He looked at me for a second, as if making a shrewd guess, then cocked his index finger at me, thumb in the air. "You thought I was an asshole with Barb."

I was not about to admit that I could be so self-righteous, but Alfred said, "Well, I was. I was. All that stuff about not wanting to marry her. Well. She didn't want to get married. And now if I wanted to go back to her, it's too late. She's going out with Mike Teutsch."

"What about Ellen?"

"Ditched me. A week ago. How's Sandy?"

"Fine. Well, fine, but we had a fight tonight."

"Women," Alfred said, maturely.

He said it as if it were plain that I knew it too, the way you might talk to a teammate and in the same tone you might use in a locker room ("Refs!").

Maybe this was just the way it was between men and women; they fought and made up and fought again, too bound up in each other to relax the way . . . the way Alfred and I were right now, sitting on the porch!

And if something seemed wrong with that as a view of human nature, it was comforting, too. A car turned onto the street and I followed it, realizing all at once that I hoped

208

it *wasn't* Sandy. For the moment I was happy to be with Alfred, friends again. Sure, I would have to make up with Sandy. But I would do it when I was good and ready.

"Yeah," I said. "They're somethin'."

○ ○ ○

She was lying on her back on a blanket on the golf course with her dress pulled up around her waist and her eyes closed. "Do it," she was saying. "Do it."

But the boy on his knees in front of her, fumbling with the blue plastic condom container, wasn't me. It was a crew-cut Gene Kleven, naked, with moles running the length of his back just the way I had noticed them when he had come out of the shower after basketball practice.

It was dark. Even though the windows were open I was sweating. I closed my eyes again; not only did I feel wide awake, I was so anxious I couldn't lie still.

Was there anything to it? I sat up and turned on the bed lamp. My watch, lying on the night table, said 2:30. Crossing the room to my desk, I looked through a stack of books for something that would take my mind off her, but there was nothing, and without Alfred around, it wasn't so easy to be calm.

Could she be on the golf course right now? After all, she would have had to get home and it would be perfectly natural for Gene to have taken her. Who knows what he would suggest with them alone again?

But that wasn't fair. Sandy had told me about Gene right from the beginning. She had been so open, I was sure I could trust the things she said ("There's nobody like you, Howie. Honestly"). Even now, hating her and hating Kleven, I knew she meant some of them. Probably she was lying awake right now, thinking about me. As I pictured her, my anger melted. I started figuring out how soon it would be proper to call her.

But calling her in the morning caused problems, too. I didn't want her coming to the game and seeing me sitting on the bench, not after the night of triumph she had had, and if that was petty of me, so what?

In fact . . . why go? Suddenly, breathtakingly, I knew I had found the solution.

Why even go to the game? Why subject myself to their meanness? Just stay home, read a book, wait for Perkins to call, and never show up for Maccabiah again! On that note I closed my eyes and, thinking it was impossible, slept again until it was nine-thirty.

After a few minutes, I swung out of bed, put on a T-shirt and bermudas, and went downstairs. My parents were sitting in the kitchen; my father was taking a bagel out of the toaster, reaching in and jabbing it tentatively with a fork as if it were a snake.

"What time is the game?" he asked.

"I'm not going."

"You what?"

"I'm not going."

"Vy not?" He had the half a bagel and put it on the plate, then picked up a knife and reached for the cream cheese.

"Why should I? I'm not playing."

The *whap* of his free hand on the Formica of the countertop startled me. "Vat you mean? So vat. You're on ze team. Zat means you show up."

I looked up. "What do you care?"

"I care. You're my son. I vant you should *act* like my son."

210

In two years he had never shown the least interest in whether I showed up at Maccabiah games. "You mean go and tell Perkins I'm sitting on the bench. Then sit and watch those clowns? After what they did?"

"Yes. Absolutely."

"Why?"

"Don't argue viz me. Just be responsible, for a change."

For a change! What did he think I was, some kind of beatnik?

Only there was something gratifying in the way he was so involved, looking right at me, holding the silver spreader motionless, one fresh morsel of cream cheese clinging to the blade. As we stared at each other it dropped off, onto the counter. He didn't notice.

"Okay," I said.

"You're going?"

"Yes."

"Good."

"Are you?"

"We'll both be there," my mother said. "Maybe, God forbid, somebody will get hurt."

40

There were new orange nets up in each goal. Hercules players were clustered around their cars at one end of the parking lot. On the grass, by the clump of trees behind the visitors' goal, were their wives, just like last time, busy spreading blankets on the grass or else on their knees in front of huge wicker baskets of food, or yelling at little kids who were in shorts and even diapers, kicking little soccer balls around.

Unlike Thursday, the stands were already half full of people, many of them the Jewish fans who were regulars and who would realize I was benched. "Get 'em, boychik," one of them said, walking by me in the parking lot.

I was too ashamed to look at him. I pretended I hadn't heard. I wished I hadn't come, whatever my orders had been.

But people had seen me already; a few of the Hercules players nodded to me as they drifted out to the field and began juggling or passing balls around. I had to walk by them to get to our team, clustered around the bench. I kept my head down. And because I couldn't meet anybody's eyes as I walked up, I was sitting down taking off my sneakers before I realized from the silence that something was going on.

It was almost exactly a replay of Thursday. Everyone was staring at me.

"It's gonna be Berger," Gatch said.

Lupo was standing next to him. But he was in street clothes—baggy chinos and, this time, a pink short-sleeved shirt open all the way down to his belt. He had a shoe on one foot, but the other, his left, was taped around the instep, the tape going up inside his pants leg.

"What happened to you?" I didn't need to ask but it seemed impudent to guess.

"Same old thing. Tore it."

Suddenly I felt weak. "How?"

"Playing with my kid."

"Doesn't matter how it happened," Gatch said. "The point is, you get your big chance today."

212

I didn't know what to say. "Well, uh, good."

But Gatch had another surprise for me. "You're in at half-back," he said.

"I'm a wing."

"Today you're a halfback. One thing you can do is run. That's been our problem all year. Nobody young enough to run. Nobody in shape enough to run. Nobody with two good legs. Today we have you and Yitzchak in there. We'll have halfbacks who can run."

For a second I wanted to object. Maybe I had looked good at halfback once or twice; I felt comfortable at wing.

"Vat's he arguing about now?" Stein called out.

"Nothing," I said.

"Okay?" Gatch said.

"Sure. Fine."

And just then I saw a fat man, bald, wearing a red, short-sleeved shirt and green plaid pants, walk over behind Gatch and stand watching us. He took a pipe out from his jacket pocket and stuck it in his mouth and began patting his pockets for a match.

41

I pretended not to see him. Coach tumbled the balls out of the mesh bag and we moved out past him and Lupo, onto the field. Was Lupo faking? I wanted desperately to ask, but there was no way to get him alone. I picked a ball out, dribbled a few steps, then rolled the ball onto my instep to juggle. That was when I realized how nervous I was; I did it so tentatively it rolled up and off the side of my foot the way it would when I was first learning the trick as an eight-year-old.

It was going to be hot. The sun was directly overhead. It wasn't even noon, but the grass was completely dry, and when the ball hit one of the worn areas in front of the goal it kicked up little puffs of dust.

By now I couldn't see Perkins. I could see my parents, sitting in the top row. I spent a minute looking over the rest of the crowd. After all, wasn't it possible Sandy would come? Now that I was playing I wished she would. But I didn't see her.

"Want to get in here?"

It was Marshak. He was standing in a circle with the other forwards.

"Sure."

They moved back, silently, to make a wider circle. Marshak passed me the ball, a little chip that I took on my thigh, dropped to the ground, and passed on.

"I want the ball a lot," he said to me, finally. "Better feed me."

He said it in a tone so hostile, as if it was all he could do to even speak to me, that I got angry too. "I'll feed you when you're open," I said.

I noticed Yitzchak looking at us. He said nothing. He never said anything to me. At first I hadn't minded because I didn't think he understood. Now, imagining that he did and that his silence implied contempt, I glared at him until he looked away.

When Gatch called us over he did it casually, and his pep talk would have sounded casual except that his voice was much louder than usual for the benefit of the people in the front rows of bleachers. "Big game," he said. His hands shoved into his rear pockets. "Everybody knows what to do. So do it. We beat these *altekockers,* we're in." He turned to me. "Howie, you played some very good ball for us all year. I know we had our differences. Our ups and downs. But we all know what a great ball player you can be. Show us."

And then it was hands in the circle, the team, I'm afraid, actually roaring, *"L'Chaim!"* and we were jogging out to our positions.

Bruch took the ball from Stein on the kickoff. He turned and, with me open and close to him, fed it to Yitzchak.

I was actually relieved. For the first time I could remember I was actually trembling when I ran. I wasn't sure I could handle a ball that came to me.

Yitzchak passed out to wing, but a Hercules player intercepted it. He stopped with the ball and passed back to his halfback.

It was so hot everybody was pacing themselves, right from the beginning. I couldn't blame them. My shirt was soaked already just from the warmup. The sun was blazingly bright; you had to squint each time you looked for a ball in the air. My face was wet and my hair hot.

"Get back. Get back! Watch feeftin," Marshak was shouting to me. I moved over, saw the pass was coming to number fifteen, broke into the opening to intercept it perfectly with my right foot, my body simply taking over. I faked number fifteen one way, then took the ball over his outstretched left foot, passed off, and suddenly I was relaxed.

Or at least I was until, after five minutes more, it had become clear that our backs weren't passing to me.

215

At first I couldn't believe it. It was just like the practice in May: whenever Goldstein or Levy got the ball they would pass to Yitzchak or else send long, booming passes downfield. I headed a goal kick. I tackled one of the Hercules halfbacks who had the ball. But over the first ten minutes I didn't get one pass.

"I'm open, I'm open," I shouted to Goldstein after—so rushed he barely had time to bring his foot back—he passed forty yards right into the chest of one of the Hercules halfbacks.

"I hear you," he said. The next time he had the ball he tried exactly the same thing.

Meanwhile, the Greeks were bringing the ball up slowly, using short passes to move around us, then passing out to the wings and having their halfbacks moving into the penalty box waiting for the cross. Usually Goldstein was there—as angry as he made me, I had to admit he was quick at reading the play—but the pressure was always on defense, and when he sent those long passes upfield their halfbacks picked them off and brought the ball up again.

Christofilakos was quick and in shape. He would move one way, drawing me out of the middle. Then he would move thirty yards back. Then he would fake a burst and stop. And pretty soon he would be free, dancing around, calling in Greek for a pass, and would get it.

It was embarrassing. And about twenty minutes into the half, the Hercules left wing, a short little man with a mustache and very hairy legs, took the ball into the corner, faked a cross to draw Goldstein out, then cut in, dribbled by Goldstein, and fed Christofilakos a little chip, which he headed down and past Rabinowitz, who, diving frantically, too late,

216

landed on his shoulder on the hard-baked ground.

Christofilakos started leaping in the air, arms over his head, legs curled beneath him. The rest of the Greeks converged on him, and they were hugging and dancing. On the sidelines twenty Greek women jumped up from their cotton bedspreads to shout in Greek.

I felt myself grabbed around the arm. It was Yitzchak. "Ve god to talk to dese guys," he said.

Sweat was pouring off his face. His hair was plastered wetly across his forehead. He looked serious.

"They won't pass to me," I said.

"I know dot," he said. With that he walked up to Marshak and said in English for my benefit, "You not passing to Howie. Dat's vy dey score."

"Ah, bullshit," Marshak said.

"*You* bullshit. *You.*"

Sirulnick, playing left inside, came over. "Yitzchak's right. We can't handle the long kicks. You're playing like high school."

Suddenly Yitzchak broke into a torrent of Yiddish. I couldn't understand a word. Marshak began yelling back at him in Yiddish.

"MARSHAK! MARSHAK!"

It was Gatch, yelling from the sideline. "Tell Goldstein to use the halfbacks!"

Marshak turned his back and went back to his position. The referee blew his whistle and motioned at us.

"Thanks," I said to Yitzchak.

He looked angry. "Azzholes," he said.

That did it. We lost the ball on the kickoff; one of their halfbacks brought the ball up, then passed to one of the

217

wings. But when he crossed it, Goldstein intercepted, and instead of heading the ball out of the penalty box, he trapped it and sent me a pass on the ground. I slowed it with the inside of my left foot, turned, faked, got by one Greek half-back, then saw Yitzchak, open, a few yards ahead of me. I passed to him.

From then on, until the half ended, I was in the play all the time. I was getting passes on the ground, passes in the air, seeing the play spread out in front of me more clearly than ever. I could see openings and wings breaking. I could read the defense. The last five minutes of the half we started getting shots. Sirulnick had one that bounced off the post; then Yitzchak took one, a long shot from outside the penalty area that curved, forcing their goalie to dive to his left and punch it over the end lines.

o   o   o

"Now you're playing like a team," Gatch told us at half time.

The older players were lying on the grass, too exhausted to move. Marshak was flat on his back, his shirt off, orange peels littering the ground beside him. Gatch spent the ten minutes moving around, bending and squatting beside one player after another, patting them on the ass or saying things too low for me to hear.

Lupo came up to me, limping. "You play gut."

I looked at him. "Is that foot . . . does it, is it really bad?"

For a second he looked angry. But he couldn't resist letting me know he had done me a favor. He grinned.

"Ah," he said. "Fuck dese assholes. I'm getting old."

We scored five minutes into the second half. The play

218

started with Yitzchak. He took a Hercules goal kick on his chest, trapped it, sent it out to Hermann at right wing. One of the Hercules fullbacks came out on Hermann. Sirulnick went right for the hole that created and headed the cross past the goalie.

Five minutes later *they* scored, on a long, curving Christofilakos shot from just inside the penalty area. About seven minutes after that we tied it up: a free kick from Yitzchak headed in by Stein. And with that Hercules brought two forwards back and began playing a stalling, defensive game aimed at a tie.

"Get the ball up there," Gatch was shouting from the sidelines, a Jewish Pat O'Brien. "We tie and they win. We tie, they *win*!"

Do you know what it's like to see a Greek midfielder trap the ball and put the sole of his foot on the ball and stand motionless while seconds tick away? To see your own guy too tired to give him the challenge that would get him moving? And then the Greek passes back to his fullback and they start little triangles of short ground passes, killing as much time as they can?

Once we did get the ball and a Greek player went down, moaning and holding his leg to fake an injury. I had time and looked up in the stands. My parents were hidden behind a group of fans standing up and yelling. Perkins was in the lowest bleacher. I could see the red shirt. He was sitting forward, head in his palms, elbows digging into his thighs.

What if he were scouting Yitzchak?

It could happen! Couldn't he suddenly see this other eighteen-year-old who for all I knew would be brilliant, a scholar whose intellect was hidden because he didn't speak

219

English and meanwhile was the best player out there? Wasn't that just the kind of classically ironic note I'd learned to expect? It wasn't enough to play well! I had to score!

I began playing out of position. If a Greek forward had the ball I would move in on him, give him a few fakes, then tackle. I made a few mistakes, but I wound up with the ball a few times, too. And once I had it I would keep it. Sweat was pouring off my face. The band of my shorts was soaked. My socks were rolled down and I didn't roll them back up.

Then, with seven minutes left, Christofilakos tried to trap a pass from one of his fullbacks and lifted his foot too high. The ball went under his foot to me. He charged me. I rolled the ball back with my cleats, out of his way; he stumbled and fell and all of a sudden I had a clear path to the goal from thirty yards out.

And in that second, the second that I saw the Greek goalie begin his move to the near post to cut off my angle, two blue and white uniforms—blue shorts, so I knew they were Greek—jerking themselves around to converge on me, the ball two yards away sitting up on the brown grass, a few scuffs the only marks on its brown and white paneling, in that moment, I saw Yitzchak break between the fullbacks, a good ten yards closer but not offside, and in midstride I changed the angle of my planted foot, turned my left foot out, and sent a pass right between the backs, on the ground, and watched him bang it in.

I hated him. He started jumping in the air just like Christofilakos. From fifty yards away Marshak found the energy to sprint across midfield and jump on Yitzchak's back. Sherman and Hermann and Sirulnick came rushing over to crowd around and pound him on the back and cup their hands around his head and shake it back and forth. The Jews in the stands were screaming words I couldn't understand. I began walking back to position.

Except then Marshak broke loose and ran over to me. "Good pez. Good pez," he said, and in spite of myself, chills went up my back. They were following him, each of the Maccabiahs, slapping me on the ass or the back, and then Yitzchak ran over to hug me.

The ref's whistle blew. Now it was our turn to fall back and play defense and now I was in almost every play. Goldstein would pass to me. I would stop the ball, look over the defense, then send a pass over to Yitzchak. Then him back to me. Me out to Marshak, and he would finally bring the ball up. The Greeks were shouting to themselves. When they got the ball they were firing shots at the goal, but they were shooting from forty yards out. We had them covered. The crowd started counting down when it was thirty seconds left. Every time I had the ball I would feel myself out of breath, my stomach and legs aching, and when I got rid of the ball I didn't think I could do it again. But then my breath would come back.

"FIVE . . . FOUR . . . THREE . . . TWO . . . ONE. . . ."

There was another ten seconds of play before the ref's whistle blew and then the crowd started running on the field toward us.

Most of them went for Yitzchak. But Gatch ran straight for me. So did Lupo, limping a little but jogging away. Behind him I saw Perkins in his red shirt, walking slowly. Behind him I saw my parents.

221

42

Gatch reached me first. He grabbed my hand with both of his, pumping it. Lupo, coming up more slowly because he had to fake the limp, pounded me on the back, and then the rest of the team was around me, shouting and pummeling me so I had to hold up my hands to protect myself.

They were saying things like, "You did it, boy!" "You came through!" in the stilted English my father sometimes used.

Then I saw the red shirt and pipe. I thought Perkins would push through the crowd and introduce himself to me. Instead he eased his way through, almost shyly, then punched Gatch on the shoulder. He had to do it twice. Gatch turned around, a little annoyed. He looked at Perkins for a second. Then he grinned. *"Walter."*

"How are you?"

"Fine. What are *you* doing here?"

"Scouting," Perkins said. Then he turned to me. "Do you know who I am?"

"Sure."

"Well, let me shake your hand. Fine game. *Fine* game. I thought you were a wing."

"He is," Gatch said. "We had an injury. You're scouting him?"

"Answer me this. Is it too late for us to get into the act?"

My heart was pounding and not because I had been running. "It's not too late," I said.

222

"Well, good."

"You'll have to talk to my father."

"Is he here?"

"I'm here," my father said.

Bruch and Stein came up, Stein grabbing my hand, saying, "Dot's my boy," as if it wasn't the first nice thing he had said to me all year. Yitzchak was courteous; it seemed incongruous even at the moment, this blocky, heavy-muscled teenager, sweat dripping off his cheeks, a dirt-streaked shirt clinging wetly to his chest, having recovered from his outburst on the field. He shook my hand and smiled. Even Marshak came up and said, "Vus gut," looking down and hurrying away.

The Greeks were heading off toward the parking lot, stripping off their shirts, holding cleats in their hands. There was a Greek family sitting on the grass near us. The wife was throwing things into the wicker basket and yelling at the kids. The Jewish fans were laughing and shouting and bunching around the players. Seeing the rest of the team crowding in, Perkins pulled my parents away from me.

"We're going over to Segal's," Gatch said. "If you want to come."

He was holding a yellow plastic pitcher.

"That's water?"

"Yes."

I took it from his hand, took a few gulps, then poured a little on my free hand and ran my hand over my neck and arms. Then I looked at him.

He knew exactly what he had said. He stood still, hands behind his back, letting just the shadow of a smile play around his lips like some college admissions counselor who had told me I'd won early admission to Cornell.

223

I stood there without answering for a second. Then I said, "I don't think that's a good idea."

"You're perfectly welcome."

Perfectly welcome! For a year I had fantasized about being invited to Segal's; about proving myself on the field enough to walk in with a bunch of the players, them laughing, punching me lightly on the shoulder, and talking about some brilliant cross or a corner kick; Gatch telling the others that he was glad he had "befriended me"; Shaw pulling a seat out at a table and sloshing beer into my glass; and later some quiet discussion about how wrong they had been to treat me like a Five Towns kid, like some soccer-playing Mort Peskin. And I knew that in the glow of winning I was supposed to overlook every injury, real or imagined.

The problem was, I didn't feel like it. "Perfectly welcome. Sure. To sit there and let everybody try to be nice after the way they were all year. You and Lupo talking English to make me feel comfortable. Sure."

"I don't think it would be so bad. Howie, you're part of our team."

"On the field."

When I saw him flinch I couldn't keep it up. "Look," I said. "I know it's not your fault. But in the spring I wanted to be invited to Segal's so *bad*. I mean it. And the guys treated me like shit. Like I was a *Nazi*."

"Oh. Now that's an exag—"

"Awright. Not a Nazi. But bad."

He weighed that for a second, then granted me a nod. "That's true. But they won't do it today."

Now Lupo came up again. "He comink?"

Gatch shrugged.

"No," I said.

"Vy not?"

"Because—"

"Because I been playing for you guys for two years and you never did it before."

Why punish Lupo, who had just helped me so enormously? Maybe I just wanted him to argue with me a little longer. But he looked at me. He pointed to my father. He, my mother, and Perkins were standing about ten yards away. Actually, my mother was standing a few feet off, by herself, as if the conversation didn't really concern her. My father was listening, his head slightly cocked, while Perkins, shorter, holding his pipe by the bowl, gesturing with it, was talking up into his ear.

"Dot's you fazzer?"

"Yes."

"I remember him. He used to play. About ten years bek. Vell. Gut game." He limped off.

That was all? Suddenly I realized that it was only in movies that winning solved everything. The gap between me and the team wasn't going to be filled by a well-played game. At that moment, Perkins caught my eye and, with an apologetic look at Gatch, motioned me over.

Maybe he had sat calmly in the bleachers while the game was on. Now, holding his pipe by the bowl and waving it around, he talked like an evangelist. Should he have looked me over before? Had he made a mistake? Hell no. After all, this was a sport didn't mean diddlysquat to the American public, not to mention Perkins' athletic director. Perkins was lucky to get any money at all for soccer, and that meant he couldn't get to every corner of the country the way Bear Bryant could. But now he'd seen me and he didn't mind saying I was one helluva player, one *hell*uva player, and

225

with my boards, if I needed money to go to St. Louis, he'd get it for me. Guaranteed.

I looked at my father. Even now he showed no excitement. He stood, slightly stooped, hands clasped behind his back, very correct.

But then he said, "Vell, if Howie wants it, he can go. He has my permission. But I think ve should talk it over first."

"By all means. Absolutely," Perkins said.

"You mean you'd let me go?"

"Yes."

"Just tell Cornell forget it and go to St. Louis after all this time? How come?"

"Vel," my father said, "vun thing is, a scholarship. But also, Mr. Perkins is right. The two years really changed you. You are hell of a player."

"Thank you," I said, trying not to show that what he said meant anything.

And now there was only one thing to do: get out of there as fast as I could and make up with Sandy.

43

Because by now I felt strong enough to do it. Couldn't I go to her house, rap on the front door, sweaty in my cleats and shorts and Maccabiah shirt, and when she got up from the piano to let me in, say, "Look. Hey. I know you're mad.

I don't blame you. I spoiled things last night. I was an asshole. But let me explain why"?

I was a boy who had just come through on a field when they were *waiting* for him to fail! Shouldn't I be able to apologize to a girl? And if I did it right, couldn't I see the hostility melt? Wouldn't Sandy reach out and take my hand and couldn't we start over again?

"Are you going home?" my father said when Perkins had left.

"No."

"Vere you going?"

"Sandy's."

"Oh. Okay." We looked at each other. I realized he must have wondered why Sandy hadn't been at the game. But all he said was, "Ve'll see you later."

This time the drive into the Five Towns was a joy: pulling the Chevy into the left lane on Peninsula, tromping down on the accelerator, and feeling it surge into passing gear as I went by older cars, the wind cool in my face, my arm dangling against the hot metal of the door. Sun glinted off marquees of the shopping centers along Broadway. As I came onto Sandy's street I slowed up, feeling the heat on my face and arm as the wind slackened. At first it looked like nobody was home. There was no car by the curb and the front door was closed.

Well, sure. Her father had the Cadillac and God alone knew where her mother was. I pulled wide to turn into the driveway.

And then I swerved back into my lane and drove by. There, far up the driveway, parked with its nose up to the garage door, was the green MG.

227

44

There was no mistaking it: It even had a new Hofstra decal on the trunk. I pulled over to the curb and turned off the engine, looking around to make sure they weren't peering out the living room window.

I knew I should just go home. Maybe it was nothing important. Maybe Kleven had to drop something off from his father. Maybe it was just a visit. Maybe he had dropped in and she hadn't wanted him there at all.

I turned the key, starting the engine again. But then my anger began building.

This was my girl friend! My steady! If I couldn't knock on her door and find her happy to see me, what was the purpose of going steady? And if this kind of reasoning overlooked a few things, I had to overlook a few more to do what I did next, which was to get out of the car, walk quickly along the driveway, stepping on the grass so I made no noise, inside the big mica boulders until one big step brought me onto the front porch. Feeling like Jack Webb, I looked inside the living room window. The room was empty.

Maybe the kitchen. Crouching down, I used my hand to vault off the porch onto the grass. I walked around to the back porch and up the stairs. The kitchen was dark too, but the back door was open. The first stair creaked. I stopped. After a minute or so I took them two at a time, tested the screen door, which swung open quietly, then took a step inside the kitchen, taking a second to adjust from the sunlight.

There were no lights on. In fact, looking down the hallway I saw there were no lights on anywhere.

Should I tiptoe upstairs to see if they were in the bedroom? The thought made me sick. If I did that, what did I do once I found them? Wasn't it best to slip back out the way I had come, drive off, and figure out what to do in the privacy of my own room?

"Okay, Howie. The fuck is this?"

From around the corner, Kleven came into the kitchen. And if I needed any confirmation about what was happening, he provided it all. He was wearing a pair of bermudas that hung low on his hips, thrown on so quickly no rim of underpants flashed above it. He had no shirt and no shoes.

"Hi," I said, feeling so weak it was an effort to stand.

"We been watching you since you pulled up, all that noise coming out of your car. Whaddaya think this is, *Dragnet*? IT'S OKAY, SAN. WE'RE TALKING." He flicked on the kitchen light.

Skulking around the side of house, tiptoeing up the backstairs, feeling clever and catlike, and they had been watching! There was a clumping on the stairs. Sandy came into the kitchen.

She was wearing bermudas, too. And a blouse. And Capezios. But her hair, usually straight, was tangled on the sides. The outline of her breasts was a little lower than usual. She wasn't wearing a bra.

We stared at each other. "What is this? What's going on?"

I said that because it was what I had rehearsed, going up the stairs. Only by now it was clear.

"Howie—" Kleven said.

"Gene, leave us," Sandy said.

"I'm not leaving. This kid is crazy, sneaking in. He—"

229

"Go upstairs. Come on."

For a second he looked like he would argue, the sophisticated college kid, surrounded by babies. Upset as I was, I was impressed that she looked firmly at him until he cocked his head to one side, shrugged, and left.

We were alone. "Sandy, you were upstairs with him. You were fucking."

She nodded. I felt like blood was draining from my body the way oil drained from the Chevy crank case.

"Why?"

"It happened last night. After you left."

"What happened."

"We . . . got together."

"What's that mean, 'got together'? What's that *mean*?"

"You know."

"No. I don't know. What's it mean?"

"Okay. We went out."

"You mean you fucked him then." I used the word because she wouldn't like it. "On the golf course. Sure."

"Okay. Yes. On the golf course. Yes. You happy?" She began to cry.

"What's going on down there?" Kleven called from upstairs.

"NOTHING."

"But why?" I said.

"Howie, you just don't forget someone when you've been going out for two years."

"But you said you loved me."

"I know. I know I did. I did. I *do.*"

"But you love him."

"You walked *out* on me last night. If you didn't walk out this wouldn't 've *hap*pened!"

230

"Oh. It's my fault. Well, I suppose you weren't talking to him before that."

"No. I wasn't."

"Or writing letters."

"That's different."

"Oh, sure. Different. Well, I should've known. Know how? Because you started wearing that ankle bracelet. The one he gave you. Oh, you didn't think I knew. But I knew."

She was surprised enough to stop crying. "Oh."

It was odd. I should have wanted her to deny it. Instead I felt a little surge of relief and triumph when she said, "Howie, I just didn't want to hurt your feelings."

"Secret letters wouldn't hurt my feelings? Saying you love me when you don't, *that* doesn't hurt my feelings? Sneaking out to the golf course the second I leave doesn't hurt my feelings?"

"Howie, please."

"You're so considerate," I said. Then I said the cruelest thing I could think of. "Your father was right."

She was sobbing so hard she couldn't say anything. She sank into one of the red plastic chairs of the dinette set, crying hard, not hiding her face, tears sliding down her face. "I'm a bad person," she moaned. "I know. I'm a bad person."

We didn't say anything for a long time. At one point I sat down, too. In my long socks and shorts I felt sticky with sweat. The kitchen wasn't air-conditioned. I could feel sweat break out on my lip and my forehead. Flies buzzed around the screens. Across the backyard you could see out to the next street. A woman was walking her dog. I could see her in sunglasses and toreador pants, stopping by a tree, waiting a few seconds, then moving on.

"How did playing go?" I asked, almost whispering.

231

"Fine. Oh, Mr. Kleven loved it. He said people were coming up to him all night."

"Great, great," I said, insincerely.

"And I talked to Mr. Perrino before I left. I'll play for him Thursday." A pause. "How was the game?"

"We won."

"Oh, *terrific.*"

"Also, Perkins came to see me. I may go to St. Louis."

"Oh, Howie. That's wonderful."

"Are you seeing him tonight?"

She looked up at me as if begging me not to ask. Finally she nodded.

"Sandy, this doesn't happen in one night. You must've been thinking about him before. And you didn't tell me."

"I wanted to see him. But you didn't want me to. You got jealous. And I . . . and I—"

"What."

"I wanted to make you happy."

"By lying to me? By getting my hopes up?"

"Howie, I didn't know what to do."

"Tell me the *truth. That's* what to do!"

"The truth hurts."

"Hurt me. You could take that."

"I can take it. I can take it. Oh, Howie, you're twisting things. It hurts me to hurt you. Oh, maybe not as much as it hurts you, but enough to put it off and—oh, Howie."

She was crying again. So was I. "Do you love him?" Even through my tears I heard how naïve that sounded, but I didn't break the sentence off.

"Do you really want me to say it?"

"Oh, Sandy."

Silence again, broken by her sniffling. She was looking

down. She brought a finger to her mouth quickly, nipping at a hangnail, then down into her lap, putting a hand around one fist.

Suddenly I had a new thought. "You really want to see us both. You want to"—I struggled, then the urge to be civilized won out—"make love to both of us?"

She looked at me. She shook her head.

"So who gets to be your friend?"

"I want to start going out with Gene."

"Oh."

"I'm sorry, Howie."

"Really?" I was testing her, hoping that somehow it was all an act.

She nodded, then looked down.

"Well. Okay. Then I'll leave."

Even then I was testing her. I stood up, pushed through the screen door, hoping she would call me back. I took the steps slowly; in my socks I made no noise. I heard a sound behind me. Hoping it might be some sort of strangled cry, I turned, but it was only the screen door closing. When I got to the driveway, walking along the line of mica boulders, I looked back. As bright as it was, the kitchen light let me see through the screen. She wasn't there.

And the fact that, as I turned back, I stumbled over the front fender of Gene's MG and nearly tripped across the line of boulders made me see what an utter fool she had made of me.

I don't want to stop seeing you, she had said. And meanwhile the secret letters! Saying she loved me while she put an ankle bracelet on as a secret sign of loyalty to Kleven, and now not waiting even one minute before racing upstairs, the distasteful job of getting rid of me over, to pull off her blouse and fall into bed with a grinning Gene Kleven! Suddenly the MG with its Hofstra sticker and canvas roof represented the smugness of a college sophomore, able to take her away because he had a father who could pay her money.

At first I thought I could let the air out of his tires. But there was too much risk in letting the car sit for five minutes, air hissing away.

And then I saw what to do and became so dizzy with excitement I could hardly muster the strength. Bending down, I picked up one of the mica boulders. Mr. Bessinger was right: It was heavy. Maneuvering my hands underneath, I lifted it above my head. The weight of it made me take a step backward before I could steady myself. I staggered around to the front of the car. I could see myself reflected in the green, gleaming fender. Bringing the boulder back a little farther behind my head, I sent it forward, like a throw-in, as hard as I could toward the windshield. For a second I thought I didn't have the strength—weren't windshields shatterproof?—but suddenly there was a splintering crash; there was a jagged hole in the windshield; the rock crashed through. Glass sprayed everywhere. I had a last glimpse of the boulder on the seat surrounded by glass fragments. Then I raced for the car.

45

Tires squealing, I followed the curb around the cul-de-sac and came back by her house with just time enough, glancing out the window, to see Kleven come running down the front steps in bermudas, barefoot, bare-chested. I braked sharply at the corner, turned onto Broadway, floored the accelerator to get through a yellow light, and then I could relax.

He wouldn't go after me! He wouldn't dare. He would be too scared of his parents. They would sweep up the glass, put the boulder back, then Kleven would head for Import Motors to replace the windshield before anyone saw, paying out of—what?—maybe his Bar Mitzvah bonds.

Traffic was light. I drove around for a while, too excited to decide anything more complicated than to follow the traffic. Then, alarmingly, the exhilaration began to fade. And at one point, waiting for a string of cars to go by, then making a turn onto Peninsula, I saw some Hewlett kids ahead of me, in a black 1950 Ford convertible, the top down, the boy's arm around some girl, and suddenly I realized I missed her.

Well, why shouldn't I? There was a lot there! There was a Senior Prom, the picture for which had just come back from the frame shop, and wasn't that a memory that was supposed to stay with you for life? There was *Year*book and *home*room and Liberace and nights on the golf course when she said things I knew she meant.

I drove toward the airport, but the traffic back from the beach was so dense it would have taken an hour to see any planes. I drove to the junior high, parked, and went into the stadium, sitting in the stands. I was alone: at the other end of the field two kids were playing stickball with a pink ball and a broom handle.

Was it possible that tonight I could put on a suit and comb my pompadour until it dangled halfway down my forehead, walk into Kleven's, just walk up to the piano in the middle of "Autumn Leaves," Five Towners in their charcoal-gray suits and silk dresses looking on astonished, and sweep her off the piano bench into my arms, winning her from Kleven in one display of boldness?

No. If boldness could do it, walking into her kitchen with Kleven's MG in the driveway would have been enough. She had seen that, felt guilty and ashamed, and still she broke up with me.

Remembering her shamed expression when I had scolded her ("Your father was right!") made me cry.

Would I ever be able to watch fireflies floating through the trees on the golf course, or let sunlight orange through my eyelids as I lay on the beach, or listen to a pianist without feeling my throat close off and my face contort and tears slide down my face?

But even as I let myself gulp and gasp, I realized it wasn't just Sandy. It was that I was alone; at some point I would have to ask girls out again, and it still petrified me. After all, Sandy had come to *me*! She had called *me*! Who could say I would be able to ask some girl out when I didn't know her answer?

I cried until I realized I was forcing it a little. Then I stopped.

In that case, who needed them? Who needed to wrestle with pain and jealousy, and the fact that one day you could share every thought with a girl and the next you couldn't even call her up? I was better off sticking to soccer. A soccer ball couldn't hurt you. A soccer ball couldn't make you cry.

In the car again, I eased the Chevy down the drive onto Broadway, cruised down some of the side streets in Woodsburgh, and finally went home, pulled into our driveway, and parked in back of the Caddy.

236

Five

46

My parents were on the front porch. I waved to them as I got out. But I couldn't bear to talk to them. Instead I walked around to the back. The old rubber ball I used to kick sat on the concrete beside the milk box. I rolled it out onto the grass and began to send little grass-cutting passes against the fence, automatically, trying not to think about anything but the ball. I took the rebound on the inside of my left foot. Rolling the ball onto my instep, I balanced it while I stood on one foot, then flipped it into the air like a flapjack and caught it on my instep again. I let the ball roll off my instep onto the grass, sent it against the fence, and took the rebound with the inside of my right foot, my weak foot.

"Here you are."

It was my father. "Hi."

"Going out with Sandy tonight?"

"No," I said.

"Oh," he said. "Gott, you played vell today."

I should have been happy. He was standing on a little patch of cement that bordered the garage. He was smiling. He was wearing a faded green pair of long pants and over that an undershirt, one of the sleeveless kind that he always wore when he was relaxed.

But I wasn't ready to forgive. What had made him change, anyway? What had happened to erase the anger he had shown me over the last two years? Something was phony here, and I was damned if I was going to feel good because he was being the proud father again, watching his son carry on the family tradition ("Gott, you played vell").

"I guess," I said.

He waited for me to amplify. I said nothing more. After a few seconds he made a motion with his hands that asked for the ball. Because it was less trouble than not doing it, I passed it to him. He took the ball up on *his* instep and cradled it, then juggled. But he tried to keep the ball too low; it bounced off his laces at an angle. He trapped it between his foot and the ground. "Haven't done zis in a few years," he said, his accent almost as thick as Marshak's.

"Lupo says that's for kids."

"Vat, chuggling?"

"Yeah. He's got a point."

"Vat point?"

"Well, you don't learn to play by yourself. You got to play with other people."

"Vell, if you vant to be a star. It's like music. You can't be a great artist viz just scales. But you have to *start* with scales. Ask Sandy."

"Well," I said. "That's what he says."

"Besides, it's fun. I used to love it. Do it for hours and hours. By the vay. I meant vat I said today. You played very vell." He passed the ball to me.

Somehow, his compliment made me remember I was angry with him. "Thank you."

"Made me vant to get out dere myself."

"You'd last about ten minutes," I said.

Did I really say it? My father cocked his head a little to one side, looking at me. "Vat?"

Did that make me feel guilty? Sure. And a little scared, too! But for once I hadn't let fear of him keep me quiet! "You'd last about ten minutes," I said.

"Vas that necessary?"

"You think you're so terrific. Two years and you don't go to one goddamn game. You tell me how wonderful Cornell is when you know I don't want to go there. Then you think you can change it around in one week? Oh boy. Boy, you've got some thinking to do."

There was silence. Then he said, "Please don't be mad at me."

His voice broke as he said it. I was so startled that, in the process of dragging the ball behind my leg, I sent it off toward the fence, trapping it when it came back.

I looked at him. He looked old but slightly defiant, as if it had cost him a lot to be so intimate.

"I just didn't want you doing things you regretted later. I didn't want you . . . wasting your life."

"Do you think I am?"

"No."

"Did you ruin yours?" I asked, meaning that if he had been smart enough to avoid mistakes, so was I.

"Well, we only have one. I never intended to spend it selling perfume."

And at that my anger died away.

"That's dumb," I said.

"Oh, I don't know."

"No. It is," I said.

241

He shrugged. "It's not worth arguing. I did it and I'm here. And you're there, and vy argue in the last month ve have together."

"What do you mean?"

"I mean in a month you'll be leaving and going twelve hundred miles away and that's the end of our family."

"Why?"

"Oh, not totally. But no more all of us under the same roof de vay vhen I grew up."

"I'll be back," I said.

"Zat's vat ve thought ven ve left Germany."

I was too surprised to answer. He almost never talked about Germany.

"Ve figured, so ve leave. Germany goes through some bad times. Maybe a var. Ve thought zat might happen. Zen ve come back, pick up vere ve left off. Big family reunion. Ze Germans forget their craziness and, I don't know. Life goes on. Only zere was no coming back because zere vas no one to come home to. I had forty-five first cousins. Forty died zere. Ven I left ve had a big party. At your grandfazzer's house vich he sold. Big vooden kegs of beer. Ve had music. People playing the piano. Dot vas the last time I saw any of zem. I don't mean St. Louis is like coming to America. But you don't just leave a place. You like the streets. You like the stores. You like your new friends. You meet, maybe, a girl there, some Baptist or vatever, and maybe after college you take a job dere and ve see you from den on, on holidays. Christmas, Easter. The Christian holidays."

I felt grown-up—as if he had decided to let me in on things he had kept hidden before—and the slightly heavy-handed way he drove his point home ("no one to come home to") bothered me only a bit.

242

"So how come it's okay now? Why don't you just tell Perkins I can't go?"

"I don't like it. But I saw how much you vant it even ven zey push you around. I'm not going to stand in your vay. You would hate me. Vat good is that?"

So that was it! He was right. In a month I was leaving, on a plane, to a city I had never seen and knew nothing about except that it was on the Mississippi, that Stan Musial lived there, and Lindbergh had named his plane for it. But I had seen kids leave the Five Towns thinking they would be back, then wind up in some bizarre place, letting us know by sending cheery notices to the alumni column ("Barry Wilensky, '52, has settled happily in Chapel Hill, N.C., with his wife, Bunnie . . ."). Couldn't that happen to me? Did I like the idea of winding up far from New York, coming back on vacations to see my parents a little more wrinkled and moving a little more slowly each time, the way it had been for Jody and his grandfather in *The Red Pony*?

I was still playing with the ball, keeping it on the ground and with my left instep guiding it smoothly around the back of my right foot. Then I would switch, moving the ball with my right instep.

And it wasn't only my parents. What about Alfred? I had gone to bed the night before confident—no! relieved!—that I had a friendship that wouldn't break up. But how could I count on it? I would have to write letters to him, and at Camp Ramah I hadn't written a single letter home until Mr. Schwartzburg took away free play privileges and made me scrub the bunk steps with a toothbrush.

And now, as the events of the summer were passing in front of me, I realized how much else I would leave behind.

I would leave the beach and the 707s bearing in over Rockaway Turnpike and Yearbook and driving my mother's Bel Air around town, eyes straight ahead as if I didn't know kids were waving to me. And sure, you could laugh at Mort Peskin and make fun of his father's Eldorado, but in the end I would also leave behind the snobbish pleasure I got from seeing the way people from Queens or Brooklyn nodded when I said I was from Cedarhurst, then changed the subject as if they didn't wish *they* lived there. Did I really want to leave all that?

Maccabiah. Now, that was more complicated. One of the points Perkins had made clear was that his "boys" played only for the school, even during the summer, something I knew anyway. I would have to drop off the team. Shouldn't it disturb me that I never sat in Segal's or had the kind of relaxed conversation with Stein or Marshak that could begin after today's game?

"Give me ze ball," my father said.

I passed it to him along the ground. He passed it back to me, easily.

I was surprised to see it didn't. I had thought if I only proved myself as a player I could make friends with them, even if I was from the Five Towns and despite the way they rallied around poor Marshak, with his lonely life held together by soccer. But the gap I had seen after the game was too big to be resolved by a game. And that made me lose interest in narrowing it.

"Vere's Sandy?" my father said.

"I don't know."

"She's coming over tonight?"

"No."

"I didn't see her at ze game."

"No."

x

244

By this time, because I was answering in monosyllables, he realized he had touched on a sensitive point. Probably he thought I was embarrassed to talk about girls with him. To show me he approved, he said "Lovely girl. Lovely." And suddenly the details of this afternoon and pain of knowing it was over swept over me.

"You don't know about life," Alfred had said, "until you go with a woman." Why didn't he mention the shame of it! The shame of even deluding myself that smashing a windshield could make up for knowing your girl was in bed with another guy! To have to face living in this town and seeing the two of them in a newly repaired MG, zooming down Central Avenue, or having to face questions about it from Mort Peskin or Mike Ciparelli ("She ditched ya? Just gave ya the old finger?"). It would be a million times better to be in St. Louis, where I could start over again, going to movies or walking across a leafy quadrangle or just possibly coming back to my dorm room with some girl who knew nothing about the clumsy things I had done in high school! And when I realized that, I knew I wanted to leave for a lot more reasons than playing soccer.

We were standing, my father and me, about five yards apart, sending the ball back and forth over the brown grass; I would meet it with the instep of my bare foot and send it back. Once in a while I would let it roll up my instep. I would balance it for a few seconds between shin and instep before letting it curl off onto the ground and sending it back.

Sure, I was leaving things behind but I was going toward something, too. Something exciting! Something with the promise of avoiding mistakes, something as fresh and clean as a soccer field seconds after the lines were laid out, while the players were in the locker room unable to kick divots

245

in the green and newly sodded grass. I wanted to go.

My father had taken the ball upon his instep, flipped it into the air, and was juggling, keeping the ball under perfect control, even with his brown wingtips and baggy pants, five, seven, nine times before letting it hit his knee and rebound in the air back to me.

I leaned back a little from the waist and headed it back to him. This time he took the ball on his thigh, looking awkward as he brought his thigh up because of his long pants, but then graceful as he cushioned the ball, then let it drop to hit off his instep.

"Go, Dad," I said.

"I don't forget a *ting*," he said, which wasn't literally true, of course, because everybody forgets things, big and small. But seeing his pride in being able to juggle reminded me that even when you were grown-up you needed moments when life seemed no more complicated than keeping a ball in the air. Suddenly it made me sad that we had allowed the gap between us to get so large, and I knew that, St. Louis or no St. Louis, this was one I wanted to close.

"We broke up," I confessed, to diminish it. "Me and Sandy. We broke up."

"You did? When?"

"This afternoon."

"Oh. I'm sorry."

"Well, no big deal," I said. "That's life."

"Maybe it's life," he said. "But life can be rough. Here."

The ball cut the grass as it came toward me. For the first time since Lupo had laughed at me for it, I flipped the ball into the air and brought a thigh up to meet it. Juggling. And as I did, feeling the ball hit my thigh, perfectly balanced, I knew how much I missed it. I felt completely in command,

246

concentrating wholly on the ball, and for a moment, anyway, I couldn't worry about Sandy or anything else.

"Thanks," I said. I couldn't look up at him, I would have lost control of the ball, but I think he got the point. Probably he didn't want to look right at me anyway.

Down to the instep. Then up into the air, turning my body away from the sun and my face toward the sky. I let the ball rebound off my forehead, letting myself take refuge in and comfort from the feeling that I could control the ball forever.

About the Author

Robert Lehrman has a B.A. from Tufts and an M.F.A. from the University of Iowa Writer's Workshop. Formerly speechwriter for two governors, he now lives with his wife, Susan Thaul, and son, Eric, in Manhattan. There, he writes executive speeches for Texaco.

His short fiction and nonfiction has appeared in *Transatlantic Review, The New York Times, St. Louis Post-Dispatch, Illinois Times,* and *WomenSports.* He is also co-author of *Doing Time: A Look at Crime and Prisons,* which received the National Council for Social Studies 1980 Notable Book Award and was named a Jane Addams Honor Book.

Juggling is his first novel.

Temple Israel
Minneapolis, Minnesota

IN MEMORY OF
CAROLYN MASLANSKY
FROM
GEORGIA & IVAN KALMAN